DYLAN THOMAS: *The Country of the Spirit*

*God is the country*
*of the spirit,*
*and each of us is given a*
*little holding of ground*
*in that country [;]*
*it is our duty*
*to explore that holding*
*to gain certain impressions*
*by such exploring,*
*to stabilise as laws*
*the most valuable of these*
*impressions, and,*
*as far as we can,*
*to abide by them.*
*It is our duty*
*to criticise,*
*for criticism is*
*the personal explanation*
*of appreciation.*

Dylan Thomas
*letter to*
*Pamela Hansford Johnson*

*Before the intellectual*
*work of conceiving and*
*understanding of*
*phenomena can set in,*
*the work of* naming *must*
*have preceded it, and have*
*reached a certain point*
*of elaboration. For it is*
*this process which*
*transforms the world of*
*sense impressions, which*
*animals also possess, into*
*a mental world, a world of*
*ideas and meanings. All*
*theoretical cognition takes*
*its departure from a world*
*already preformed by*
*language; the scientist,*
*the historian, even the*
*philosopher, lives with his*
*objects only as language*
*presents them to him.*

Ernst Cassirer
*Language and Myth*

# DYLAN THOMAS:

## The Country of the Spirit

ℜ Rushworth M. Kidder

PRINCETON UNIVERSITY PRESS

Publication of this book
has been aided by
the Research Committee of
Wichita State University.

This book is composed in
Linotype Caledonia

Printed in the United States
of America
by Princeton University Press,
Princeton, New Jersey

*for Liz,*
*Heather,*
*and Abby*

The major thesis behind this book, which came to me rather suddenly one Sunday afternoon, is a simple one: there are three types of religious imagery discernible in Dylan Thomas' poetry. The years of writing and revising since that Sunday have been given to explaining and illustrating this central idea. The resulting book has, like its thesis, three main divisions. The first deals with the phenomenon of religious poetry in general, establishing definitions basic to the study and examining, through Thomas' letters and critical statements, what he understood to be his own position in regard to religious poetry. The second part of the book describes and exemplifies three types of religious imagery —which I have called the referential, the allusive, and the thematic—found in his poems. The third section applies these distinctions to an analysis of his five published volumes of poetry. It is my hope that the analyses will illuminate obscure areas of Thomas' work, and that, by permitting clear distinctions between religious and non-religious matters, they will provide a coherent view of the whole body of his poetry. I hope, too, that this method will suggest a useful approach to the work of other poets who, like Thomas, have used Biblical imagery for purposes other than the simply religious.

There are many to whom great thanks are due: to various members of the faculty of Columbia University, and especially to William York Tindall, who inspired my initial interest in Thomas and advised the dissertation from which this book has grown, and to John Unterecker, from whose insights into modern poetry I have greatly benefitted, and whose encouragement gave me the conviction to persist; to Tom F. Driver of Union Theological Seminary, who with pleasant acuity taught me to ask "So what?" and thereby challenged me to think not simply of the accuracy but of the usefulness of each critical statement; to John Roderick Davis and Richard B. Davidson, for listening patiently to and conversing intelligently with me as the work progressed; to Mr. and Mrs. R. W. Davidson for their confident and unstinting support of this project in its early stages; to William Howarth of Princeton University, whose careful reading of the manuscript and perceptive suggestions for its improvement solved problems that I sensed but could not define; to Charlotte DeMoss Miller and Carol Ann Vaughan, who have assisted this work in ways no average typist could; to students, colleagues, and friends too numerous to mention, whose insights have given substance to this study; and to the many scholars who, in the forty years since Thomas began publishing, have contributed to what has already become an outstanding body of literary criticism.

I especially wish to acknowledge the generous support of the Research Committee of Wichita State University, which has funded the preparation and publication of this book. And my great gratitude goes to my wife and daughters, whose patient understanding has strengthened my hand for this work, and to whom it is dedicated.

*Wichita, Kansas*
*July 1972*

# 🐾 Acknowledgments

Permission to quote from various writings has been kindly granted by the following:

Oxford University Press. *The Poems of Gerard Manley Hopkins*, ed. Gardener & MacKenzie.

J. M. Dent & Sons Ltd. *The Collected Poems of Dylan Thomas*. Copyright © 1952 by J. M. Dent & Sons, Ltd. *Portrait of the Artist as a Young Dog*. Copyright © 1940 by J. M. Dent & Sons, Ltd. *Selected Letters of Dylan Thomas*. Copyright © 1966 by J. M. Dent & Sons, Ltd.

The Macmillan Company. "A Prayer for my Daughter," *Collected Poems by William Butler Yeats*. Copyright © The Macmillan Company.

Harcourt Brace Jovanovich, Inc.: "Ash Wednesday," by *T. S. Eliot, Collected Poems*, 1909-1962. Copyright © Harcourt Brace Jovanovich, Inc.

New Directions Publishing Corporation: *The Poems of Dylan Thomas*. Copyright 1939, 1943, 1946 by New Directions Publishing Corporation. Copyright 1952 by Dylan Thomas. *Adventures in the Skin Trade*, by Dylan Thomas. Copyright © 1955 by New Directions Publishing Corporation. *Selected Letters*, by Dylan Thomas. Copyright © 1965, 1966 and by the Trustees for the Copyrights of Dylan Thomas. *Portrait of the Artist as a Young Dog*. Copyright © 1940 by New Directions Publishing Corporation. Reprinted by permission of New Directions Publishing Corporation.

# ๑ Contents

*PART ONE*   The Mazes of His Praise

Religious Poetry

Dylan Thomas wrote religious poetry. This state-
ment has the support of a number of his critics; as it
stands, it is perfectly true and not very useful.[1] The
word "religious" has become a catchword, a simple
term of classification for certain easily observed charac-
teristics of a poem. And, as such, it has suffered from
generalization and from a tendency to subsume into it
the more specific meanings included in such words as
pantheistic, pagan, mystic, and sacramental. If the
phrase "religious poetry" is to be a part of our critical
vocabulary—and it is a very useful phrase—some clari-
fication is necessary.

The extent of this problem is indicated by the
breadth of twentieth-century commentary on the rela-

[1] "The religious element in Thomas' poetry is the key to its
correct interpretation": John Ackerman, *Dylan Thomas: His
Life and Work* (London, 1964), p. 3. "Thomas was essentially
a religious poet . . .": T. H. Jones, *Dylan Thomas* (New York,
1963), p. 66. "His perspectives are themselves those of religious
insight": D. S. Savage, "The Poetry of Dylan Thomas," *Dylan
Thomas: The Legend and the Poet*, ed. E. W. Tedlock (Lon-
don, 1960), p. 143 (hereafter cited as Tedlock). "His knowl-
edge of the Bible, and his fundamentally religious—emotionally
rather than intellectually religious—attitude to life were typically
Welsh . . .": G. S. Fraser, "Dylan Thomas," *A Casebook on
Dylan Thomas*, ed. John Malcolm Brinnin (New York, 1960),
p. 37 (hereafter cited as *Casebook*). "Thomas is a fundamentally
religious poet, and not one who uses religious and Christian
symbols merely as an additional embellishment to his verse":
Aneirin Talfan Davies, *Dylan: Druid of the Broken Body* (Lon-
don, 1964), p. 51. This list could readily be expanded.

tionships between poetry and religion. The distinct and firmly rooted views of Dr. Johnson, who held that poetry was of little use to religion, and of Matthew Arnold, who held that poetry replaced religion, have exfoliated into a tangle of more recent aesthetic and theological theorizing. Two major branches may be discerned. There are those who, with Santayana, feel that "religion and poetry are identical in essence, and differ merely in the way in which they are attached to practical affairs."[2] Along this line, David Jones argues that, since art is symbolic and symbols sacred, "Art knows only a 'sacred' activity."[3] Proponents of this view hold that the Christian cultural tradition, having shaped the work of every present-day western artist, is bound to manifest itself in western art: "it is increasingly recognized," asserts John McGill Krumm, "that an expression of cultural creativity is almost inevitably religious in its scope and ambition."[4] Not merely religious, such expression is held to be frankly Christian. For the influence of Christianity is radical enough to destroy previous faith. As C. S. Lewis quips, "A post-Christian man is not a Pagan; you might as well think that a married woman recovers her virginity by divorce."[5]

Such a view leads, inevitably, to a blurring of the

[2] George Santayana, *Interpretations of Religion and Poetry* (New York, 1918), p. v.

[3] "Art and Sacrament: An Enquiry Concerning the Arts of Man and the Christian Commitment to Sacrament in Relation to Contemporary Technocracy," in Nathan A. Scott, ed., *The New Orpheus* (New York, 1964), p. 35.

[4] "Theology and Literature: The Terms of the Dialogue on the Modern Scene," in Nathan A. Scott, Jr., ed., *The Climate of Faith in Modern Literature* (New York, 1964), p. 20.

[5] Quoted by Krumm, *op.cit.*, p. 36.

*4*

boundaries between the religious and the secular. If poetry by its very nature is religious, "religious poetry" is no more than a redundancy, and students of it no more than theoreticians of the obvious. But the fact remains that the word "religious" has implications that "poetry" does not have. And so, not surprisingly, the other major trend of thinking on this subject seeks to define the distinctions between these terms.[6] From this point of view, as Amos Wilder observes, those who would identify poetry with religion are perpetrators of "popular misconceptions" which "fall commonly into two types": "There is the mystical or spiritualist view that all poetry is religious. . . . The difficulty with such a view is that significant religion is too often confused with partial or shallow levels of experience; often with thrills, gratifications, moods which do not claim the deeper personal life. In the second place, there is the moralizing or didactic view that poetry is religious when it deals explicitly with God, Christ, Scripture, ideals or conduct, and that all other poetry is merely secular, pretty, frivolous or even immoral. Such popular misconceptions rest as much upon erroneous views of religion as of poetry."[7] The key to resolving these "misconceptions" is to be found, according to Wilder, in an adequate view of religion.

*Religion* has been defined as "a series of acts and observances, the correct performance of which was

[6] See, for example, E. I. Watkin, *Poets and Mystics* (London, 1953), p. 12; William T. Noon, S.J., *Poetry and Prayer* (New Brunswick, N.J., 1967), pp. 3-29; Helen Gardner, *Religion and Literature* (London, 1971), pp. 121-142.

[7] *Modern Poetry and the Christian Tradition* (New York, 1952), pp. 1-2.

necessary or desirable to secure the favour of the gods or to avert their anger."[8] *Webster's Third New International Dictionary* adds to this notion of performance a concomitant belief, defining religion as "The personal commitment to and serving of God or a god with worshipful devotion." Sir James Frazer remarks on this twofold distinction: "By religion, then, I understand a propitiation or conciliation of powers superior to man which are believed to direct and control the course of nature and of human life. Thus defined, religion consists of two elements, a theoretical and a practical, namely, a belief in powers higher than man and an attempt to propitiate or please them."[9] *Religion*, adequately defined, includes not only passive belief but also active participation. Paul Tillich, while insisting that the language and methods of philosophy have made invaluable contributions to the study of religion, distinguishes between philosophy and religion on precisely this ground of active engagement. Philosophy he defines as "that cognitive endeavor in which the question of being is asked."[10] Religion, more than a process of questioning, belongs with revelation to the realm of the active. Revelation, according to Tillich, "must be received, and the name for the reception of revelation is 'religion.'" He continues: ". . . revelation becomes more revealing the more it speaks to man in his concrete situation, to the special receptivity of his

[8] Robertson Smith, *The Religion of the Semites.* Quoted by H. Wheeler Robinson, *Inspiration and Revelation in the Old Testament* (London, 1946), p. 78.

[9] *The Golden Bough* (New York, 1922), p. 50.

[10] *Biblical Religion and the Search for Ultimate Reality* (Chicago, 1955), p. 5. D. G. James makes a similar point in *Scepticism and Poetry: An Essay on the Poetic Imagination* (London, 1937), pp. 242-274.

6

mind, to the special conditions of his society, and to the special historical period. Revelation is never revelation in general, however universal its claim may be. It is always revelation for someone and for a group in a definite environment, under unique circumstances."[11] Most of Dylan Thomas' critics, responding to the immense collection of Biblical references and allusions in his poetry with the label "religious," mean, by that, poetry influenced by Biblical religion.[12] And the Bible, more than a collection of convenient symbols and tales, provides its readers with attitudes as well: attitudes not only of thought but of action. Words and works, thoughts and acts, are united in Biblical religion: "Commit thy works unto the Lord, and thy thoughts shall be established" (Proverbs 16:3), says the Old Testament, and the author of Hebrews (13:16) rephrases this ubiquitous dictum as "to do good and to communicate forget not." G. Ernest Wright, in an excellent argument for the serious interpretation of the

[11] Tillich, p. 3.

[12] Thomas was acquainted with forms of worship other than Biblical. Several of his book reviews indicate an awareness of the content of the Upanishads: see, for example, his review of M. K. Ghandi's *Songs from Prison* in *The Adelphi*, IX (January 1935), 255-256, and his review of Alfred Hy. Haffenden's *Dictator in Freedom: Tract Four* in *The Adelphi*, IX (February 1935), 317-318. H. H. Kleinman, in *The Religious Sonnets of Dylan Thomas* (Berkeley, 1963), has demonstrated convincingly that the ninth sonnet of "Altarwise by owl-light" makes use of material from the Egyptian *Book of the Dead*, which Thomas may have encountered in E. A. Wallis Budge's *The Mummy* (London, 1925), a study of Egyptian burial customs. However, Thomas' critics are right in considering Biblical religion as the central religious influence. While an interesting study could be done on the influence in Thomas' work of other religions, this study will restrict itself to Biblical religion.

Old Testament as an essential element of Christianity, observes that "The word is certainly present in the Scripture, but it is rarely, if ever, dissociated from the Act; instead it is the accompaniment of the Act."[13] In basic agreement with Tillich's understanding of the historical nature of revelation, Wright continues: "It is . . . the objectivity of God's historical acts which are the focus of attention, not the subjectivity of inner, emotional, diffuse and mystical experience. Inner revelation is thus concrete and definite, since it is always correlated with a historical act of God which is the primary locus of concentration."[14] The active presence of God, as revealed in the Bible, does not permit reduction to a set of principles or ideas that exist in thought only; Biblical religion is not doctrine. "The relation between God and man," writes Emil Brunner, ". . . is not of such kind that doctrine can adequately express it in abstract formulas. . . . It is not a timeless or static relation, arising from the world of ideas—and only for such is doctrine an adequate form: rather the relation is an event, and hence narration is the proper form to describe it. The decisive word-form in the language of the Bible is not the substantive, as in Greek, but the verb, the word of action. . . . God 'steps' into the world, into relation with men. . . . He acts always in relation *to them*, and He always *acts*."[15]

[13] *God Who Acts: Biblical Theology as Recital* (Chicago, 1952), p. 12.

[14] *Ibid.*, p. 55.

[15] Emil Brunner, *Truth as Encounter*, trans. Amandus W. Loos and David Cairns (Philadelphia, 1964), pp. 87-88; quoted by Wright, *God Who Acts*, p. 90. Thorleif Boman, in a fine study of language and thought in the Old Testament, summarizes his findings in this way: "If Israelite thinking is to be characterized, it is obvious first to call it dynamic, vigorous, pas-

If religion implies action as well as belief, it also implies something beyond either. Religion insists on the kind of commitment that, not simply active, is obligatory and binding. The words *religion* and *obligation* share a common root that means "a binding"; David Jones notes that "The same root is in 'ligament,' a binding which supports an organ and assures that organ its freedom of use as part of a body." The word *religious*, then, "refers to a binding, a securing. Like the ligament, it secures a freedom to function. The binding makes possible the freedom."[16] Belief, after all, may be confused with mere superficial lip-service, the kind of "self-satisfied ventilation of fervent sentiments" that, as Mary Baker Eddy incisively remarked, "never makes a Christian."[17] Acts alone, without distinguished motives to impel them, similarly fail to determine religion: ". . . though I bestow all my goods to feed the poor," as Paul writes, "and though I give my body to be burned, and have not charity, it profiteth me nothing." Beyond belief and action there remains the essential obligation. It is this obligation that Helen Gardner, in her essay "Religious Poetry: A Definition," takes as the defining factor of religion: "Religion is more than attitudes, aspirations, emotions, speculations and intimations. Although it can include all these things, it includes them within a way of life consciously accepted in obedience to what are felt to be imperatives

---

sionate, and sometimes quite explosive in kind; correspondingly Greek thinking is static, peaceful, moderate, and harmonious in kind." *Hebrew Thought Compared with Greek*, trans. Jules L. Moreau (Philadelphia, 1960), p. 27.

[16] "Art and Sacrament," pp. 36-37.

[17] *Science and Health with Key to the Scriptures* (Boston, 1906), p. 7.

from without the self that are binding. It expresses itself, and has throughout all ages and in all societies, in rituals that have to be performed and in rules of conduct that are obligatory both personally and socially."[18] Wilder includes these three aspects of belief, obligation, and action in his definition of *religion* as "our relation to the 'unconditioned' or ultimate, or that which has unconditional obligation for us, together with our response to it."[19]

The phrase "religious poetry" will be of greatest consequence here if it is defined in terms of Biblical religion, and if Biblical religion is understood to entail participation and obligation as well as theory. Religious poetry, then, will be found to involve (1) statements about faith based on Biblical thought, (2) a sense of obligation, and (3) a sense of active participation. It must be made clear, however, that obligation and active participation are *not* defined by membership in a particular church or sect; the question of the religious nature of a poet's work cannot be resolved simply by a biographical investigation into his form of worship. Nor are they defined by the poet's adherence to publicly accepted codes of behavior. Whether activity and obligation are public or private—whether the poet's public morals are consistent with what others consider to be the standard of public morality—is not in issue here.[20] Poetry, to be religious, must be so not

---

[18] *Religion and Literature*, p. 134.

[19] *Modern Poetry and the Christian Tradition*, p. 3.

[20] John Malcolm Brinnin writes that "many people found it difficult to connect [Thomas] with the poems he wrote. But, as he said, they would have felt the same sort of consternation, the same disbelief—'How could such a man have written such marvelous devotional poems? I saw him fall downstairs in his

as a result of what is read into it from the facts of a poet's life, country, or social milieu; it must be so by virtue of its own statements, by the language the poet uses to determine his thought and the thought that is expressed through his language. Active participation involves a concept of religion as something other than philosophy, or ethics, or morality, or social decorum. Obligation demands both a commitment to faith and a course of activity consonant with and responsible to that commitment. These must occur where they matter most: in the privacy of the poet's work.

That Thomas considered poetry an active endeavor is apparent from his metaphors for the creation of a poem. Song, he said in the "Author's Prologue" to *Collected Poems*, is "a burning and crested act" (p. xv).[21] The materials from which song (poetry) is constructed are words; and words are substance. They can be "sawn," and the poet can "hack" them into a "rumpus of shapes" (p. xvi). Hardly a passive process, his "craft or sullen art" demands that he "labour by singing light" (p. 142). His labor results in such tangible products as the "hewn coils of his trade" (p. 190) and the "skyward statue"—the memorial for Ann Jones—that is "carved from her in a room with a wet window" (pp. 96-97). Throughout his work the fashioning of poetry is compared to sculpturing, woodworking, and tailoring; metaphors for words include stone, wood, and cloth. Answering some questions about his poetic method, he

---

suspenders'—had they met some of the famous dead." *Dylan Thomas in America: An Intimate Journal* (New York, 1955), p. 57. "They have their reward," says Jesus (Matthew 6:5) in condemnation of those who confuse prayer with public display.

[21] Page numbers in parentheses refer to Dylan Thomas, *The Collected Poems of Dylan Thomas* (New York, 1957).

summarized his metaphors of word-as-substance in this way: "What I like to do is to treat words as a craftsman does his wood or stone or what-have-you, to hew, carve, mould, coil, polish and plane them into patterns, sequences, sculptures, fugues of sound. . . ."[22]

Thomas' concept of poetry as an active endeavor found its clearest expression in a little-known review that he wrote for *The Adelphi*. Commenting on J. W. Tibble's edition of *The Poems of John Clare*, he observed that ". . . the best of Clare becomes both social and universal poetry, and . . . even at his worst, he had none of the private, masturbatory preoccupation of the compulsive egoist. To Clare the writing of poetry was an action. Poetry, to too many, is a mental accident, or a substitute for physical expression. And though Clare's physical life was bounded, for the most part, by the walls of an asylum, he was an 'active' poet, just as Keats, despite his enduring passion, was a man who acted life through poetry."[23] Action, for Thomas, was necessary in poetry. Somehow the words had to come to life of themselves, had to convey something more than a cognitive meaning. A profound involvement in the poetic medium was, he felt, essential. Noting that "all writers either work towards or away from words," he explained to Pamela Hansford Johnson that "The realistic novelist—Bennett, for instance—sees things, hears things, imagines things (& all things of the material world or the materially cerebral world), & then goes towards words as the most suitable medium through which to express these experiences. A romanticist like Shelley, on the other hand, is his medium first,

[22] Dylan Thomas, "Poetic Manifesto," *Texas Quarterly*, IV (Winter 1961), 46.

[23] *The Adelphi*, x (June 1935), 180.

12

& expresses out of his medium what he sees, hears, thinks, & imagines."[24] For poetry, as he later wrote to Charles Fisher, ". . . should work from words from the substance of words and the rhythm of substantial words set together, not towards words. Poetry is a medium. . . ."[25]

The question to be asked, then, is: What means did Dylan Thomas use to create active poetry? The answer, simple to phrase, is of complex significance, his most frequent activity, and the means through which he participated in poetry as well as in religion, was the activity of praise.

The language of praise forms a basic element in almost all of Thomas' poetry. Praise, however, is not prayer. These two words, although often conflated, arise from distinct roots and have distinct meanings.[26] Praise often forms a part of prayers; the Lord's Prayer, mainly a supplication, begins with praise. But to praise is to extol or magnify; to pray is to beseech or request. Praise includes selfless adoration inspired by the worth of the praised object or person; prayer often implies a subjective involvement inspired by need. True praise is freely given, with no thought of any return; true

[24] Letter dated "2nd May, 1934," in *Selected Letters of Dylan Thomas*, ed. Constantine FitzGibbon (New York, 1967), p. 115. This volume is hereafter cited as *Letters*.

[25] "February 1935," *Letters*, p. 151.

[26] "Pray," according to the *Oxford English Dictionary*, derives from the Latin *precari*, meaning to entreat or supplicate; it is related to the word "precarious," whose first meaning is "Held by the favour and at the pleasure of another; hence, uncertain." "Praise," on the other hand, derives from the Latin *pretium*, meaning value or price, and is related to the word "prize." In its earliest English use, it means to appraise, value, or esteem. Prayer, then, involves the concept of request; praise involves the concept of worth.

*13*

prayer is a request for a return. These statements, not intended to denigrate prayer, point to the radical distinction between praise and prayer, a distinction made in the interests of recovering the individual value of these words and of restoring each to a useful place in our critical vocabulary.

As is the case with the word "religious," such distinctions have not always been observed by Thomas' critics. T. S. Eliot, in a very different context, once noted that "the essential of any important heresy is not simply that it is wrong; it is that it is partly right."[27] One of the important heresies in Thomas criticism is expressed by statements such as "Poetry to him is prayer."[28] Partly right, this statement probably arises from a confusion of "praise" and "prayer," the sort of confusion that can occur in a reading of lines such as

> O may my heart's truth
>> Still be sung
> On this high hill in a year's turning.
>> ("Poem in October," p. 115)

These lines are clearly prayer; yet they involve praise. The poet prays that next year he may be able to sing such praise as he has just finished singing this year. But to define Thomas' poetry as prayer, because it includes prayer from time to time, is not simply to fall victim to the notion that the only true religious act is prayer; it is also to ignore the great number of his poems that, thick with religious imagery, make no re-

[27] After Strange Gods: A Primer of Modern Heresy (London, 1934), p. 26.

[28] Edith Sitwell, in The Atlantic Book of British and American Poetry, ed. Edith Sitwell (Boston, 1958), p. 982. Quoted in Casebook, p. 125.

14

quests. More useful statements are that praise constitutes, for Thomas, a religious act, and that praise is the essence of his poetry.

From the beginning to the end of his poetic career, Thomas conceived of poetry not only as praise, but as praise of God. As early as 1933, when he was nineteen years old and had just begun to publish, he wrote to Pamela Hansford Johnson: "It is said to be mad to write poetry. . . . But . . . Art is praise and it is sane to praise, for, praising, we praise the godliness that gives us sanity. . . ."[29] And two years before his death, after his greatest poems of praise had been written, he ended a nine-page statement about his poetic principles with this sentence: "The joy and function of poetry is, and was, the celebration of man, which is also the celebration of God."[30] Praise is the subject of the famous "Note" that prefaces *Collected Poems*: "I read somewhere of a shepherd who, when asked why he made, from within fairy rings, ritual observances to the moon to protect his flocks, replied: 'I'd be a damn' fool if I didn't!' These poems, with all their crudities, doubts, and confusions, are written for the love of Man and in praise of God, and I'd be a damn' fool if they weren't" (p. xiii). This note bears an ironic disguise, an attempt to confound a serious interpretation of realized truth by clothing it in mockery and humor; so does the quip (attributed to Thomas by Brinnin) that he intended to produce "poems in praise of God's world by a man who doesn't believe in God."[31] These statements suggest two important characteristics of Thomas' poetry: the concept that poetry is praise, and the complemen-

[29] "25th December 1933," *Letters*, p. 83.
[30] "Poetic Manifesto," p. 53.
[31] *Dylan Thomas in America*, p. 128.

*15*

tary notion that such a concept, too fragile for direct communication, must be packaged in a protective ambiguity that takes either the form of irony (as it does here) or the form of verbal opacity (as it does in many of Thomas' early poems). These two characteristics, praise and poetic ambiguity, are closely related. The existence of one helps explain the reason for the other. The attempt to account for the relationship between praise and ambiguity, however, has spawned a number of critical epithets, four of which—mystic, sacramental, pantheistic, and pagan—arise in response to Thomas' ambiguity and occasion some obscurity of their own.

The poetry of Dylan Thomas has been called mystical.[32] This word, helpful in an approach to some of his poems, deserves clarification. It does not simply mean occultism (of which there is very little in Thomas' work), nor does it simply mean a symbolism that poetically expresses the occult. It is not a general term for transcendental philosophy, nor is it a specific term for sentimentality or enigma. At its simplest, it is, in D. G. James's words, "the movement of the imagination to penetrate to what is beyond our world."[33] According

[32] "The truths of Thomas' images are not those of ordinary experience, but those of his mysticism": Jacob Korg, *Dylan Thomas* (New York, 1964), p. 42. "Primarily he believed, like all mystics from the Druids to Blake, in an essential Unity of Being": Clara Lander, "With Welsh and Reverent Rook: The Biblical Element in Dylan Thomas," *Queen's Quarterly*, LXV (Autumn 1958), 445. "Thomas moves between sexual revulsion and sexual ecstasy, between puritanism and mysticism": Karl Shapiro, "Dylan Thomas," in Tedlock, p. 277. The notion is popular enough that *Time*, in Thomas' obituary, referred to him as "Wales' bright young mystic of English poetry . . .": November 16, 1953, p. 93.

[33] *Scepticism and Poetry*, p. 261.

to its great apologist, Evelyn Underhill, it is "the expression of the innate tendency of the human spirit towards complete harmony with the transcendental order."[34] According to Miss Underhill, this "innate tendency" may be cultivated by a systematic approach to contemplation that involves four specific characteristics. In the first place, mysticism concerns the spiritual and the transcendental; it has no particular concern with the visible universe. Unlike Thomas' poems, mystic expression is not visceral, sexual, or social. Although involved totally with the self, mysticism does not look down the avenues of the senses, but up into another dimension of being. In the second place, mysticism is an active undertaking; it is, in the terms developed earlier in this chapter, religious rather than philosophical in its nature. The mystic, according to Helen C. White, strives "to focus all his resources upon his main purpose of coming into contact with his God."[35] As a result of this emphasis on activity, the mystic One is, thirdly, interpreted as a personal, living being, not simply a passive object that is to be explored and defined; love, and not intellection, is the mystic's goal. Fourth, the approach to this One is a definite, particularized process known as the Mystic Way. The resulting union, a "state or form of enhanced life," entails a "complete remaking of character and the liberation of a new, or rather latent, form of consciousness."[36]

[34] *Mysticism: A Study in the Nature and Development of Man's Spiritual Consciousness* (London, 1911), p. x. I am indebted to Miss Underhill's work throughout this discussion.

[35] *The Metaphysical Poets: A Study in Religious Experience* (New York, 1936), pp. 11-12.

[36] Underhill, p. 96.

*17*

Thomas, not a dogmatic poet, nor one to accept a doctrinal view of life, apparently never ventured into the Mystic Way, nor did he attempt to remake his character in accordance with mystic principles. He was nevertheless concerned with aspects of transcendental harmony, especially insofar as this harmony is expressed in the relation of self to God. Too committed to the evidence of the senses to ignore materiality, however, his poetry can be considered mystic (and then only occasionally) only in the broadest sense of an "innate *tendency* of the human spirit," rather than in the specific terms of the Mystic Way.

Just as mysticism may be a contributory, but not a defining, attitude in Thomas' poetics, so the concept of sacrament, a part of a larger whole, does not define the whole. Critics have called attention to the sacramental aspects of his poetry.[37] They usually refer either to (1) Eucharistic symbols or references, or (2) ritualistic form in the structure and language of a poem. There is a great deal of ritual in Thomas' poetry, especially in such later poems as "After the funeral," "A

[37] "A metaphor for Thomas was sacramental: it was a symbol and a reality, both, and simultaneously": Moynihan, *The Craft and Art of Dylan Thomas* (Ithaca, New York, 1966), p. 224. "It is the sacramental side of Christianity which appears to have appealed to him most": Thomas Saunders, "Religious Elements in the Poetry of Dylan Thomas," *Dalhousie Review*, LXV (Winter 1965-1966), 495. "It is obvious that he finds the sacramental approach increasingly congenial, and as he developed, we see him take over, more and more, a Catholic imagery and symbolism": Davies, *Dylan: Druid of the Broken Body*, p. 21. David Daiches notes that "A Refusal to Mourn" is "ritualistic in tone; its dominant images are sacramental": Daiches, in *Dylan Thomas: A Collection of Critical Essays*, ed. C. B. Cox (Englewood Cliffs, N.J., 1966), p. 18.

Refusal to Mourn," "Ceremony After a Fire Raid," and "Over Sir John's hill." More than ritual, however, a sacrament is primarily, in Webster's definition, "A religious act, ceremony, or practice that is considered especially sacred as a sign or symbol of a deeper reality." Biblical religion is a necessary constituent of this definition; there are moments of unreligious ritual and ceremony in Thomas' earlier poems (the best example is probably "Especially when the October wind"), but, lacking explicit reference to Biblical religion, these would not be understood, in any ordinary sense, as sacramental. The word "sacrament" will be most helpful when used to define aspects of Thomas' poetic language and structure that, referring to Biblical religion, call attention to the poem itself as an *act* of ceremony or celebration, an act that signifies, while simultaneously drawing its power from, a transcendent dimension of reality.

Dylan Thomas has also been accused of pantheism and pagan primitivism.[38] These appraisals, not unpredictable for a poet who makes such statements as

[38] "His religion became . . . a blending of his indigenous paganism and those aspects of Christianity which he found most acceptable": Stuart Holroyd, "Dylan Thomas and the Religion of the Instinctive Life," *Casebook*, p. 148. "The universe which is both the subject and the setting of Thomas' early poetry and short stories is a rediscovery of the reality found in primitive religion": Korg, *Dylan Thomas*, p. 29. "Thomas is a primitive poet, and the cost of that primitive celebration is the loss of the civilized virtues and the problems of civilized men": William Arrowsmith, "The Wisdom of Poetry," *Casebook*, p. 101. David Daiches contrasts early and late work by stating that Thomas progressed ". . . to a period of more limpid, open-worked poetry in which, instead of endeavoring to leap outside time into a pantheistic cosmos beyond the dimensions, he

> The force that through the green fuse drives the flower
> Drives my green age; that blasts the roots of trees
> Is my destroyer                                    (p. 10)

and who further asserts that "The country is holy" (p. 182), are insufficient. It is not that they are untrue; like Eliot's heresies, they are partly right. But they do not do justice either to Thomas' poetry or to his poetic intentions.

Pantheism is a belief in the unity of creation; it is "the doctrine that all things and beings are modes, attributes, or appearances of one single reality or being; hence nature and God are believed to be identical."[39] It is one extreme of the distinction between immanence and transcendence, the other extreme being deism.[40] In popular usage, it often comes to mean an

---

accepts time and change . . .": "The Poetry of Dylan Thomas," in Cox, p. 22. Stanley Moss notes Thomas' "subjective half-pagan pantheism" ("Fallen Angel," *The New Republic*, June 10, 1967, p. 20); and William York Tindall remarks his sense of "the holiness of nature—in Wordsworth's pantheistic sense or Lawrence's . . ." (*A Reader's Guide to Dylan Thomas* [New York, 1962], p. 274).

[39] Van A. Harvey, *A Handbook of Theological Terms* (New York, 1964), p. 173. See also G. Ernest Wright's definition of pantheism as a doctrine "in which the divine is believed to be immanent in the evolving process, a principle, whether personalized or impersonal, pulsating through the movement of nature and giving it form and coherence." ("The Faith of Israel," in *The Interpreter's Bible* [New York, 1952-1957], I [1952], 365.) For further distinctions between Oriental panentheism and pantheism, see Hoxie Neale Fairchild, *Religious Trends in English Poetry*, vol. VI (New York, 1968), p. 409.

[40] ". . . in pantheism the deity is wholly immanent, in deism . . . it is wholly transcendent, and in theism . . . it is both transcendent and immanent." *A Handbook of Theological Terms*, p. 235.

ecstatic and unreasoned union with living nature; poetically, it lurks in the same bushes as does surrealism, and ultimates in what has been labeled "the cult of the irrational."[41] Pantheism, generally an uncomplicated doctrine, was not, for Thomas, a satisfactory approach to his world. A deity wholly immanent is a deity wholly knowable—a claim Thomas rarely cared to make. He did claim, in a letter to Trevor Hughes, that it was his aim as an artist ". . . to prove beyond doubt to myself that the flesh that covers me is the flesh that covers the sun, that the blood in my lungs is the blood that goes up and down a tree. It is the simplicity of religion."[42] Such a statement, necessary evidence to establish pantheism, is not sufficient evidence: unity of body and nature is not unity of man and nature, nor is it unity of God and nature. Pantheism was a familiar word to Thomas. He speaks (a little glibly, to be sure) of Wordsworth as "a human nannygoat with a pantheistic obsession."[43] And in his radio talk "How to be a Poet," he describes, with a withering humor, his conception of the pantheistic poem:

"It is, of course, about Nature; it confesses a wish to escape from humdrum routine and embrace the unsophisticated life of the farm labourer; [the poet] desires, though without scandal, to wake up with the birds; he expresses the opinion that a ploughshare, not a pen, best fits his little strength; a decorous pantheist, he is one with the rill, the rhyming mill, the rosy-bottomed milkmaid, the russet-cheeked rat-catcher, swains, swine, pipits, pippins. You can smell the country in

[41] Amos N. Wilder, *The Spiritual Aspects of the New Poetry* (New York, 1940), pp. 113-140.

[42] "12th January 1934," *Letters*, p. 87.

[43] "Undated, probably September 1933," *Letters*, p. 24.

his poems, the fields, the flowers, the armpits of Tripto-
lemus, the barns, the pyres, the hay, and, most of all,
the corn."[44]

William Moynihan, noting very rightly that "the
beginning of Thomas' antipantheism is a misconception,
an identification of pantheism with the pathetic fal-
lacy," provides a cogent assessment of Thomas' reac-
tion to pantheism, and returns us to the idea of poetry
as activity: "Pantheism seemed to Thomas an involve-
ment with life at a lesser stage of being, at a lesser stage
of intensity. In pantheism, Thomas felt, all the poten-
tialities of man were not realized. In Thomas' canon
there had to be thought, not a rational process but
some vital activity which, to Thomas, was equivalent
to thought. . . ."[45]

The objection to paganism resembles the objection
to pantheism: both are static attitudes that, once ac-
cepted, lead out to no further dimensions of reality.
In polytheistic, pagan faiths, according to G. Ernest
Wright, "The order of nature was believed to be an
achievement in the integration of divine wills, in the
pairing of complementary powers by means of the
family and household patterns, and in the balancing
of opposing forces such as life and death, rain and
drought. The life of the individual was embedded in
society and society was embedded in the rhythm and
balance of nature which was the realm of the gods.
The whole aim of existence was thus to fit into the
rhythm and integration of the cosmic society of na-
ture. . . . Polytheism was thus pre-eminently a religion

[44] *A Prospect of the Sea and Other Stories and Prose Writings*
(London, 1955), pp. 105-106.

[45] *The Craft and Art of Dylan Thomas*, p. 35.

of the *status quo*. . . ."[46] One important result of such a belief, a result that opposes it to Biblical belief, is that ". . . the pagan religions have no sense of history. Polytheistic man, borne on the rhythmic cycle of nature, has no primary concern with history; instead his focus of attention is upon the yearly cycle in which life is re-created each spring and the blessing of order re-established."[47]

It may be observed that Thomas' poetry is full of cycles: of birth, death, and rebirth; of spring, fall, and another spring; of love, anger, and love again. For Thomas, however, life consists in rising above the small cycles and recognizing the larger history—especially the Judeo-Christian history, with its examples of Adam, Noah, Abraham, Moses, and Jesus—that helped form the civilization around him. The cycle of the seasons, insistent though it is, must not be accepted, for it implies death:

> . . . seasons must be challenged or they totter
> Into a chiming quarter
> Where, punctual as death, we ring the stars.
>
> (p. 2)

In "Altarwise by owl-light" the poet, in the "half-way house" of life between birth and death, is not content with passive existence bounded by these ultimates; he reconstructs a kind of miniature world history, a "Christian voyage," in these ten sonnets, and ends by holding, "Atlaswise," his world "half-way off the dummy bay," committed to neither extreme and rising above both. In "Vision and Prayer" the birth and rebirth imagery does involve the poet in repetition; but, not merely sea-

[46] *God Who Acts*, p. 20.    [47] *Ibid.*, p. 24.

sonal, this repetition is the grand Christian cycle, the reincarnation of faith at a specific point in history, determined not by earthly revolution but by divine revelation.

Thomas' most specific rejection of paganism, however, is embodied in his feelings about Lawrence. To Pamela Hansford Johnson he wrote: "Lawrence preached paganism, and paganism, as the life by the body in the body for the body, is a doctrine that contents man with his lot. It defies the brain, and it is only through the brain that man can realise the chaos of civilisation and attempt to better it."[48] While "the life by the body in the body for the body" defines something less than the extensive pattern of Wright's paganism, this reaction against animality placed Thomas in sympathy with Christian attitudes. He was even willing to declare this preference publicly: "Lawrence is hard to find. He was primarily concerned with the achievement of a pagan content. There is no pagan literature. The brains of man cannot lead his body to a pagan nirvana. . . . The state of pagan bliss produces nothing but pagan children, a brood contented with the social purpose of any civilisation so long as their hot and seedy streams do not dry up. The state of Christhood produces a love-dictated progeny and a communal art."[49]

On the one hand, then, pantheism limits man's vision of the potentialities of life; on the other, paganism limits the potentialities of his mind. Thomas, too active a poet to abide either restriction, and too dynamic to

[48] "Late 1933 (?)," *Letters*, p. 71.

[49] Review of *Dictator in Freedom: Tract Four*, by Alfred Hy. Haffenden, in *The Adelphi*, ix (February 1935), 317.

tolerate acceptance of the *status quo*, rejected the doctrine of each while making use of elements from both.

If "pagan" and "pantheistic" are incorrect, and "mystic" and "sacramental" are inconclusive, why have these labels been so frequently applied to describe Thomas' poetry? The answer is to be found in the obscurity that appears to characterize much of Thomas' poetic language. These labels probably arise in a reader's mind as a result of feeling rather than meaning. A poem, syntactically opaque or structurally incoherent, can nevertheless—through the impression made on its readers by isolated images or phrases—have about it an aura of meaning, something that gives rise to a feeling that there is, beyond the limits of its understandable imagery, a greater sense. Such a poem will appear to have a mysterious incomprehensibility built into it. If the understandable imagery is religious, these four labels will seem appropriate. If the mystery in the poem suggests arcane religious practices, the words "pagan" or "mystic" will seem to fit. If the mystery suggests some transcendental and emotional significance of the things of the world, the words "pantheistic" or "sacramental" will seem apt. Facing obscurity that seems to be religious, the reader may respond to its tone with one of these labels. Such labeling, often arising from frustration rather than definition, suggests that the central challenge of Thomas' poetry is its ambiguity. It is to this problem that the following chapter addresses itself.

"If Mr. Wordsworth is not equally with [Samuel] Daniel alike intelligible to all readers of average understanding in all passages of his works, the comparative difficulty does not arise from the greater impurity of the ore, but from the nature and uses of the metal." Thus Coleridge defends his friend against charges of obscure writing, continuing, "A poem is not necessarily obscure, because it does not aim to be popular. It is enough, if a work be perspicuous to those for whom it is written. . . ."[1] Thomas' poetry, defendant against similar charges, benefits by Coleridge's insights. To say that his substance is contaminated and his medium unrefined is inadequate. It is rather that his product, which does not "aim to be popular" in the sense, say, of Kipling's product, is being put to use in a very special way: it is exploring the emotional and intellectual relationship of the poet to his God in a dimension so individual and so far removed from the merely "popular" that no simple reading can do it justice. Recognizing the significance of this religious dimension—correctly assessing "the nature and uses of the metal"—the reader of a Thomas poem joins "those for whom it is written" and is better able to resolve the obscure into the perspicuous.

Obscurity is not to be confused with ambiguity. Ambiguity, as William Empson has explained, properly

[1] *Biographia Literaria*, ed. J. Shawcross (London, 1907), II, 120.

belongs to the author's domain; it arises as a result of his own undertaking.[2] Obscurity, on the other hand, is best used to describe a result of the reader's response —or, at times, the failure of his response—to poetic language. Ambiguous statements may cause some obscurity; but, while many poets have cultivated ambiguity, few have cultivated deliberate obscurity. Obscurity, since it is commonly the reader's problem, has as its antidote a clarification of the reader's way of thinking. This clarification is usually effected by a certain familiarity with a poet's work. Once we have read enough, we begin to understand the poet's particular language and his individual use of ambiguity; we begin, that is, to "catch on." Catching on properly explains the process: we catch hold of something, anything, that promises to make sense of the poem, and, using this one particular sense as a handle, we pull ourselves further into the poem and begin to elaborate other senses.[3]

There are varieties of poetic obscurity. Eliot, to avoid causing an obscurity of allusion and reference,

[2] "We call it ambiguous, I think, when we recognize that there could be a puzzle as to what the author meant, in that alternative views might be taken without sheer misreading": William Empson, *Seven Types of Ambiguity*, 2nd ed. (London, 1947), p. x.

[3] As an example of how "catching on" involves dispelling obscurity by finding even one meaning for a complex poem, compare the various interpretations of "Altarwise by owl-light." Olson caught hold of astrology; Tindall caught hold of the portrait-of-the-artist theme; Kleinman caught hold of religious allegory. These views, each of which makes sense, are not mutually exclusive: each serves the invaluable function of allowing the reader to say, "The poem, at least, means this"—a point from which he can go on and say, "The poem, also, means this and this."

found it necessary to attach footnotes to *The Waste Land*. Assuming, correctly, that his readers would be puzzled by suggestions of Dante, Baudelaire, Ovid, Shakespeare, and a host of others—and further assuming that their puzzlement would lead to obscurity—he provided essential information. Hart Crane's poetry, having a similar allusive obscurity, demands of its readers a knowledge of a different sort. Acquaintance with the New York City landscape, with its Statue of Liberty and its Wall Street, resolves some of the obscurity attending the phrases ". . . the chained bay waters Liberty" and "Down Wall, from girder into street . . ."; the opening of "The River" section of *The Bridge*, clotted with trade-names and advertising slogans, appears opaque unless the reader knows that "Tintex," "Japalac," and what follows are actual examples of the "patent name on the signboard."[4]

Yeats's poetry best exemplifies another sort of obscurity. In contrast to much of contemporary writing, there are few lines or phrases in Yeats's work that seem, even at first reading, incomprehensible. But while sentences or verse paragraphs make, in themselves, clear and understandable statements, the relationship between such units is often obscured. What, for example, is the connection between "hysterical women," Shakespearean characters, "Old civilisations," and the three Chinamen in "Lapis Lazuli," or between children, Helen, Plato, Aristotle, and dancing in "Among School Children"?[5] This is not obscurity of reference: identifying Helen or Cordelia, while helpful, does not make the relationship apparent. Until the reader undertakes

[4] *The Bridge* (New York, 1930), pp. 7, 8, 22.
[5] *The Collected Poems of W. B. Yeats*, Definitive Edition (New York, 1956), pp. 291-293 and 212-214.

28

to integrate these parts and define their relationship, the poems as completed works of art remain obscure.

Still another sort of obscurity involves the poet's multidimensional use of individual words. It frequently arises when the ambiguity of a pun appears in such a way that the second meaning, the punned meaning, of the word makes more immediate sense than the word's face value. Readers of Wallace Stevens, finding this obscurity, are driven to the dictionary. There they can discover, for example, that "An Ordinary Evening in New Haven" makes sense when "ordinary" is taken to mean a tavern or dining room.[6] Similarly, E. E. Cummings' "anyone lived in a pretty how town" seems obscure until "anyone" is seen as the proper name of an individual character.[7]

This consideration of an obscurity due to grammar suggests another sort of obscurity, an obscurity due to syntactical dissociation. The reader of Hopkins, coming upon the following lines in "The Wreck of the Deutschland," will want to stop and parse what he has read before he tries to discover its meaning:

> . . . Oh,
> We lash with the best or worst
> Word last! How a lush-kept plush-capped sloe
> Will, mouthed to flesh-burst
> Gush!—flush the man, the being with it, sour or sweet,
> Brim, in a flash, full!—Hither then, last or first,
> To hero of Calvary, Christ, 's feet—
> Never ask if meaning it, wanting it, warned of it—men go.[8]

[6] *The Collected Poems of Wallace Stevens* (New York, 1954), p. 465.

[7] E. E. Cummings, *Poems: 1923-1954* (New York, 1954), p. 370.

[8] *The Poems of Gerard Manley Hopkins*, ed. W. H. Gardener and N. H. MacKenzie, 4th ed. (London, 1967), p. 54.

29

These lines, which appear obscure partly because of punctuation—how many sentences are involved here? —also demand that the comparison between the "sloe" and the "hero" be understood. Similarly obscure is this sentence:

> . . . Manshape, that shone
> Sheer off, disseveral, a star, ' death blots black out;
> Is any of him at all so stark        [nor mark
> But vastness blurs and time beats level.[9]

Understanding depends on identifying the referent of "him," and of the interpretation of "mark" as noun or verb; it also depends on the realization that "disseveral," a portmanteau word, combines "dissever" with "several."

All of these varieties of obscurity plague our understanding of Dylan Thomas' poetry. Since he was not a scholar, and since he spent more of his time studying his own words for the world than he did studying the words of others, the obscurity caused by reference or allusion to uncommon things is limited. His poems, however, like those of Yeats, often demand that the reader resolve relationships between plain (and sometimes not-so-plain) statements; why, for example, are the "holy face," the reasoning of the heart, and the ball in the park all parts of the poem "Should lanterns shine" (p. 72)? Like Stevens, Thomas makes use of puns, secondary meanings, and grammatical disruptions: "The scaled sea-sawers" (p. 83) is a phrase loaded with the various meanings of "scale" and the puns on "sea" and "saw"; and the line "There must, be praised, some certainty" (p. 56), is a shorthand that means something

---

[9] "That Nature is a Heraclitean Fire and of the comfort of the Resurrection," *ibid.*, p. 105.

like "There must be (God be praised) some certainty." Syntactical dissociation, however, far exceeding that of Hopkins, causes the greatest obscurity: the first twenty-five line sentence of "When, like a running grave" (p. 21)—which is not the most difficult example of Thomas' syntax—leads through a puzzle of punctuation and a variety of verb-forms before the elements can be correctly parsed and the meaning determined.

The foregoing discussion presumes a definition of poetry. One of the tenets of this definition requires that a poem, to be a satisfactory work of art, integrate all the elements of its composition into a unified structure; it is the tenet expressed by Conrad's famous statement that "A work that aspires, however humbly, to the condition of art should carry its justification in every line."[10] The poem must account for every word and every rhythm: nothing can be extra, nothing can be out of place, nothing essential can be missing. It is because of this requirement for unity that the reader, encountering a poem and making the assumption that it *is* a poem, has the responsibility of penetrating obscurity and understanding the relationships among all the parts—all the allusions, connections, verbal ambiguities, and syntactical complexities—of a poem.

"Making the assumption that it *is* a poem" suggests one of the greatest obstacles to the reading of contemporary poetry. It is a necessary assumption. If the poet has not done his work properly, obscurity cannot be resolved, parts will not relate, and unity will not be achieved. The verse will not be poetry, and nothing the reader can do will make it so. Before engaging himself in this industrious work of resolving obscurity, then, the

[10] Preface to *The Nigger of the Narcissus* (New York, 1914), p. 11.

reader would like assurances that his labor will not be in vain. Here reputation—for better or for worse—plays a great part: the reader will perhaps be more willing to extend himself for a reading of a Thomas poem than for a reading of a poem by a relatively unknown poet. The point of this discussion is that everything an author writes affects everything else he has written. We are more willing to trust his craftsmanship in one particular poem—and, consequently, to labor over its apparent obscurity—if we know the poet to be a responsible, capable, careful craftsman in his other poems.

Dylan Thomas, no obscurantist, was that sort of careful craftsman. "Poems," he said publicly, "are pieces of hard craftsmanship made interesting . . . by the work put into them."[11] What he called the "texture" of a poem—the technique by which words are made into poetry—was of primary importance. Definitions of poetry can include statements about meaning and feeling; but for Thomas the essential tenet (as he wrote to Margaret Taylor) concerned technique: "The *meaning* of a poem you cannot, as a poet, talk about in any way constructively: that must be left to theoreticians, logicians, philosophers, sentimentalists, etc. It is only the *texture* of a poem that can be discussed at all. Nobody, I think, wants to talk, either, about how a poem *feels* to him; he finds it emotionally moving or he doesn't; and, if he does, there's nothing to discuss except the means, the words themselves, by which this emotional feeling was aroused."[12] This texture was not, for Thomas, the result of surrealism, or of any uncontrolled uprush of subconscious thoughts. Instead, it was highly disciplined.

[11] "Questionnaire: The Cost of Letters," *Horizon*, xiv (September 1946), 174.
[12] "Late 1945," *Letters*, p. 285.

When he wrote to Richard Church that he had never been, "never will be, or could be for that matter, a surrealist," he entered a plea against the charge of obscurity in his own poetry: "Every line *is* meant to be understood; the reader *is* meant to understand every poem by thinking and feeling about it, and not by sucking it in through his pores, or whatever he is meant to do with surrealist writing."[13] And fifteen years later he responded to a question about his relationship to surrealism with a statement insisting on control and order: "I do not mind from where the images of a poem are dragged up; drag them up, if you like, from the nethermost sea of the hidden self; but, before they reach paper, they must go through all the rational processes of the intellect."[14]

The label that Thomas chose to express his notion of the perfect integration of all the elements of a poem was "inevitability"; in a good poem, every word appears inevitable. In the course of a lengthy correspondence with the Welsh poet Vernon Watkins, Thomas, responding to one of Watkins' poems, invoked this concept of inevitability and the congruent concept that a successful poem is an active, not a passive, creation: "All the words [in your poem] are lovely, but they *seem* so *chosen*, not struck out. I can see the sensitive picking of words, but none of the strong, inevitable pulling that makes a poem an event, a happening, an action perhaps, not a still-life or an experience put down, placed, regulated. . . ."[15] An inevitable poem, into which the poet

---

[13] "9th December 1935," *Letters*, p. 161.
[14] "Poetic Manifesto," *Texas Quarterly*, p. 52.
[15] "[Undated: envelope dated 21st March 1938]," *Dylan Thomas: Letters to Vernon Watkins*, ed. Vernon Watkins (London, 1957), p. 38. This volume is hereafter cited as *Watkins*.

has put all his effort, remains an active creation because it demands response. It is not a closed, finished, static object, for "however taut, inevitably in order, a good poem may appear, it must be so constructed that it is wide open, at any second, to receive the accidental miracle which makes a work of craftsmanship a work of art."[16]

The method of constructing such a poem is one of Thomas' central concerns. His reply to Watkins' criticism of "Once it was the colour of saying" (p. 98) stresses the complete integration of form and substance that he demanded in poetry: "I see your argument about the error of shape, but the form was consistently emotional and I can't change it without a change of heart."[17] This devotion to craftsmanship of shape and statement militates against any idea of Thomas as a poet of obscurity: he was a poet of ambiguity, but his intention was constantly directed at a communication, not a misunderstanding, between reader and poet. Again and again he pleaded for a "literal" reading of his poems. To Henry Treece he wrote: "I ask only that my poetry should be taken literally";[18] and in a later letter he objected to Edith Sitwell's interpretation of the opening lines of "Altarwise by owl-light" on the grounds that "she doesn't take the literal meaning."[19] A literal reading, however, is not to be confused with a simple reading. Thomas, aware of the difficulties of his own poems, dismissed Pamela Hansford Johnson's belief that a good poem is a simple poem with the reply: "that all good poetry is necessarily simple seems to me

[16] "Questionnaire: The Cost of Letters," *Horizon*, p. 174.
[17] "Sunday [January 1939 . . .]," *Watkins*, p. 53.
[18] "16th May 1938," *Letters*, p. 196.
[19] "1st June 1938," *Letters*, p. 198.

very absurd. . . . It is the simplicity of the human mind
that believes the universal mind to be as simple."[20] To
Richard Church, who had asked him to send a group
of "more-or-less simple, unambiguous poems" for pub-
lication, he replied as he had replied to Miss Johnson:
simplicity was not, for him, a worthwhile criterion.
"Just as you, as you said, would consider it almost dis-
honest to publish poems you could not explain to those
people who might buy them, so I feel it would be dis-
honest of me to attempt to get published a complete
book of 'simple poems'; I shall always go on trying to
write simple, unambiguous things, but they can only
be a very little part of my work. . . ."[21]

"There must be," he wrote to Miss Johnson, "no
compromise; there is always the one right word. . . ."[22]
Such statements as these, finally, make a reading of
Thomas' poems easier. They go a long way towards
dispelling the idea of persistent, intentional obscurity.
They establish in principle what his poems established
in fact: poetry, for Thomas, was a "craft or sullen art"
in which everything that was used—even ambiguity—
had a reason and a place.

What is the place of ambiguity in Thomas' work?
The answer to this question is intimately related to the
answer to another question: what is the place of re-
ligion in his work?[23] Sir James Frazer made an observa-

[20] "Late October 1933," *Letters*, pp. 37, 38.
[21] "17th March 1936," *Letters*, p. 168.
[22] "Undated, probably September 1933," *Letters*, pp. 23-24.
[23] A relationship between ambiguity and religious concerns
is by no means unique to Thomas. Nathan Scott suggests that
the ambiguity of modern literature is due to the "metaphysical
isolation" of the modern artist, who experiences "a great lone-
liness" in that he is "unaided by ministeries either of Church
or of culture." This loneliness "is unquestionably the reason

*35*

tion about the nature of worship that aptly describes Thomas' relationship to formal religious practice. Noting that "it is not necessary that religious practice should always take the form of ritual," Frazer observed that religious practice is intended "to please the deity, and if the deity is one who delights in charity and mercy and purity more than in oblations of blood, the chanting of hymns, and the fumes of incense, his worshippers will best please him, not by prostrating themselves before him, by intoning his praises, and by filling his temples with costly gifts, but by being pure and merciful and charitable towards men. . . ."[24]

Thomas, "charitable towards men" and a worshipper in his own way, was not a conventional churchgoer. Raised in the traditions of the Welsh chapel, he was not exactly an attentive pupil of its religion. Speaking autobiographically, the mature Thomas recalls the young boy in the schoolroom who "scuffled at prayers" and "interpolated, smugly, the time-honoured wrong / irreverent words into the morning hymns."[25] His father had, apparently, "decided that there was no God."[26] But his mother, and her side of the family, remained well with-

---

for the obscurity of so many great modern texts. . . . For, amid the confusion of values of this age, the artist is attempting to invent a system of attitudes and beliefs that will give meaning to his world. And it is this idiosyncrasy, this extreme individuality, of modern poetic vision that has often made our finest literature so difficult to penetrate." *The Broken Center: Studies in the Theological Horizon of Modern Literature* (New Haven, 1966), p. 8.

[24] *The Golden Bough*, pp. 50-51.

[25] "Return Journey," *Quite Early One Morning* (London, 1954), p. 84.

[26] Constantine FitzGibbon, *The Life of Dylan Thomas* (London, 1965), p. 13.

in the fold of conventional Welsh Nonconformity. Bill
Read, one of Thomas' friends and biographers, reports
that: "Dylan's grandfather was a deacon, his Uncle
Tom Williams was a Swansea preacher, and his Uncle
David Rees became a well-known figure as minister of
the Church of the Paraclete in Newton, a position he
held from 1898 until 1933. Dylan, his mother, and his
older sister Nancy all attended the Congregational
Church, where Dylan earned the Sunday School certifi-
cate he kept on the wall of his room. When they went
to visit Aunt Dosie and Uncle Dai on week ends, as they
often did, everyone went to church services three times
a day at the Paraclete: morning services at eleven,
Sunday school at two-thirty, and evening services at
six-thirty."[27] His exposure to the chapel, as extensive as
it was, did not imbue him with the conventional spirit.
Living in a society that countenanced only strict ad-
herence to its Nonconformist ethic, he managed to
avoid becoming a Christian by simple osmosis. His
response to the Welsh Bethel, not as vitriolic a reaction
as that of writers such as Caradoc Evans or D. H. Law-
rence, was nevertheless a more gentle indictment of
the hypocrisy, complacency, and selfishness which they
found there.

In *Apocalypse*—a strange, personal blend of scholar-
ship and vendetta that concerns The Revelation of St.
John the Divine—D. H. Lawrence describes his own
experience as a Nonconformist child: "From earliest
years right into manhood, like any other nonconformist
child I had the Bible poured every day into my helpless
consciousness, till there came almost a saturation point.
Long before one could think or even vaguely under-
stand, this Bible language, these 'portions' of the Bible

[27] *The Days of Dylan Thomas* (New York, 1964), p. 24.

were *douched* over the mind and consciousness, till they became soaked in, they became an influence which affected all the processes of emotion and thought. So that today, although I have 'forgotten' my Bible, I need only begin to read a chapter to realise that I 'know' it with an almost nauseating fixity."[28] The Book of Revelation, according to Lawrence, was "on the face of it a grandiose scheme for wiping out and annihilating everybody who wasn't of the elect, the chosen people. . . ."[29] Chapel people, he said, took over this plan, seeing themselves as "chosen people." What Lawrence calls "the Christianity of tenderness" was, in Nonconformity, "utterly pushed aside by the Christianity of self-glorification: the self-glorification of the humble."[30]

Thomas, voicing similar observations in a more amused manner, concentrated on the countryside as well as its inhabitants. He described "Blaen Cwm, Llangain, Carmarthenshire, Wales" as a place "where the Bible opens itself at Revelations," and where, as he writes to Oscar Williams, "I went to the Edwinsford arms, a sabbath-dark bar with a stag's head over the Gents and a stuffed salmon caught by Shem. . . . I rode back on a bicycle through the justice-must-be-done-let's-rain-on-sinners rain. . . ."[31] Describing to Miss Johnson a Sunday in Wales, he depicts the "Sunday-walkers" who "like a river end up in the sabbath well where the corpses of strangled preachers, promising all their days of a heaven they don't believe in to people who won't go there, float and hide truth."[32] But the finest expression of his feelings about Welsh Noncon-

[28] D. H. Lawrence, *Apocalypse* (New York, 1966), pp. 3-4.
[29] *Ibid.*, p. 13.           [30] *Ibid.*, p. 16.
[31] "July 30, 1945," *Letters*, pp. 278, 280-281.
[32] "15th April 1934," *Letters*, p. 102.

formity is the portrait of "cousin Gwilym" in the short
story "The Peaches." With superb humor—a humor
not made bitter with sarcasm and satire, but rather
made gentle through compassion and understanding—
Thomas describes Gwilym, who is "studying to be a
minister," as "a tall young man aged nearly twenty,
with a thin stick of a body and a spade-shaped face.
You could dig a garden with him."[33] Gwilym, "dressed
in minister's black, though it was a weekday morning,"
leads the young narrator to his makeshift chapel in the
barn and delivers, with the requisite Welsh *hwyl*, a
sermon.

"I sat on the hay and stared at Gwilym preaching,
and heard his voice rise and crack and sink to a whisper
and break into singing and Welsh and ring triumphant-
ly and be wild and meek. The sun, through a hole,
shone on his praying shoulders, and he said: 'O God,
Thou art everywhere all the time, in the dew of the
morning, in the frost of the evening, in the field and
the town, in the preacher and the sinner, in the sparrow
and the big buzzard. Thou canst see everything, right
down deep in our hearts; Thou canst see us when the
sun is gone; Thou canst see us when there aren't any
stars, in the gravy blackness, in the deep, deep, deep
pit; Thou canst see and spy and watch us all the time,
in the little black corners, in the big cowboys' prairies,
under the blankets when we're snoring fast, in the ter-
rible shadows, pitch black, pitch black; Thou canst see
everything we do, in the night and the day, in the day
and the night, everything, everything; Thou canst see
all the time. O God, mun, you're like a bloody cat.' "[34]

[33] *Portrait of the Artist as a Young Dog* (London, 1940),
pp. 14, 16.
[34] *Ibid.*, pp. 21-22.

Later, with a friend, the narrator discusses Gwilym:
"Jack's tears had dried. 'I don't like Gwilym, he's barmy.'

" 'No, he isn't. I found a lot of poems in his bedroom once. They were all written to girls. And he showed them to me afterwards, and he'd changed all the girls' names to God.'

" 'He's religious.'

" 'No he isn't, he goes with actresses. . . .' "[35]

Because he saw the churches breeding the pantheistic confusion of people like Gwilym, Thomas, in serious as well as in humorous moments, had little faith in institutionalized religion. "Everything is wrong that forbids the freedom of the individual," he wrote to Miss Johnson; "the churches are wrong, because they standardize our gods, because they label our morals, because they laud the death of a vanished Christ, and fear the crying of the new Christ in the wilderness."[36] To a man unconcerned with Christianity, these considerations of church and morality would be of little interest. Thomas, however, returned to these topics again and again. In an earlier letter to Miss Johnson, after stating his belief that "every thinking man . . . gradually forms a series of laws for living . . . ," he continued with a rare personal statement about his interpretation of Christianity:

"Jesus was himself a critic more than anything else; he was given God to read, he read God, understood Him, appreciated Him, and then, stern in his duty as a critic, decided it was his mission in life to explain the meaning of God to his fellows.

[35] *Ibid.*, p. 35.
[36] "11th November 1933," *Letters*, p. 64.

"God is the country of the spirit, and each of us is given a little holding of ground in that country[;] it is our duty to explore that holding to gain certain impressions by such exploring, to stabilise as laws the most valuable of these impressions, and, as far as we can, to abide by them. It is our duty to criticise, for criticism is the personal explanation of appreciation."[37]

Using "criticism" in the sense of "evaluation" or "analysis," Thomas here states in religious terms what he frequently stated in literary terms: "criticism is the personal explanation of appreciation." Moreover, he recognizes his duty not only to appreciate God but to communicate that appreciation. And the most effective way to communicate appreciation is to praise.

Although his praise is generally a praise of the body, it insists on the fact that the body is God's. Seeing himself as a type of Christ, a Christian surgeon-healer who is "all glory's sawbones" (p. 84), Thomas attempts in poetry what Jesus manifested in life: a raising of the dead and an overcoming of death. It is his "positivity of faith and belief" that supports him: "so many modern poets," he complained to Miss Johnson, "take the *living* flesh as their object, and, by their clever dissecting, turn it into a carcase. I prefer to take the *dead* flesh, and, by any positivity of faith and belief that is in me, build up a *living* flesh from it."[38] For, as he later wrote in Biblically simple language, "a live body is a building around a soul, and a dead body a building without it. . . ."[39]

His belief in praise was an active one; it was, in its own way, a religion. Its effect on him was a desire to

[37] "October ? 1933," *Letters*, pp. 28-29.
[38] "Late 1933," *Letters*, p. 74.
[39] "25th December 1933," *Letters*, p. 82.

*41*

act, to do, to create. Sometimes, as in the following sentences to Miss Johnson, his language evinces a desire for an action of moral significance: "I want to believe, to believe for ever, that heaven is *being*, a state of being, and the only hell is the hell of myself. I want to burn hell with its own flames."[40] Sometimes the desire is for a proper language, a correct way of expressing within his mind (and, consequently, of seeing) ultimate beauty: "Now there is nothing on God's earth that is, in itself, an ugly thing; it is the sickness of the mind that turns a thing sick and the dirtiness of the mind that turns a thing dirty."[41] On one occasion at least, the language burst the bounds of private correspondence and struck out publicly for his beliefs: he wrote the editor of the *Swansea and West Wales Guardian* that, to combat "humbug and smug respectability," the readers of that newspaper must be told of "the undeniable conviction that the divinity of man is not to be trifled with, that the manna of God is not the lukewarm soup and starch of the chapel, but the red-hot grains of love and life distributed equally and impartially among us all. . . ."[42]

Much later, in recollecting the dominant influences on his work, Thomas made what is probably the fairest assessment of his debt to the Bible: "Its great stories, of Noah, Jonah, Lot, Moses, Jacob, David, Solomon and a thousand more, I had, of course, known from very early youth; the great rhythms had rolled over me from the Welsh pulpits; and I had read, for myself, from Job and Ecclesiastes; and the story of the New Testament is part of my life. But I have never sat down and studied the Bible, never consciously echoed its lan-

[40] *Ibid.*, p. 84.      [41] *Ibid.*, p. 82.
[42] "14th January 1934," *Letters*, p. 93.

guage, and am, in reality, as ignorant of it as most brought-up Christians. All of the Bible that I use in my work is remembered from childhood, and is the common property of all who were brought up in English-speaking communities."[43] Whether this is completely true or not—and if it is, he had an almost incredible memory for proper names and detailed narratives in the Bible—it indicates Thomas' consciousness of the Bible's influence in his work. Not only in his work, however, was the Bible an influence. From the statements in his letters—as well as those, more complex, in his poetry—it is not hard to believe his assertion that "the New Testament"—the basis of Christianity—"is part of my life."

To affirm Biblical religion in these terms is, for Thomas, to make a remarkably unambiguous statement. Feeling this way, why did he not say so plainly in his poetry? Or (to phrase this question in terms less personal and more literary), what can be said of the relationship between ambiguity and religion? For a poet of Thomas' caliber and craftsmanship, such a question defies simple answers. Ambiguity is a major aspect of his style, and religion is a major aspect of his thought; to inquire into the relationship between them is to inquire into the very heart of his poetry. This inquiry is best pursued by an analysis of those points in the poems—the religious images themselves—which fuse religious significance with ambiguous statement.

Speaking of Thomas' poetry, Ralph Maud notes that "the task the poet sets himself" is "to express the important and intimate facts of experience without seeming to blurt them out."[44] He achieves distance through

[43] "Poetic Manifesto," *Texas Quarterly*, p. 49.
[44] *Entrances to Dylan Thomas' Poetry* (Pittsburgh, 1963), p. 81.

ambiguity; and "the final aim of distancing"—the aim of that tremendous complexity of syntax and sense which Thomas erects—is "not to obscure, but to prevent us from rushing in with the hackneyed, with our own notions rather than the poet's."[45] This distance seems to come most frequently in conjunction with religious poems; which, perhaps, is another way of saying that many of Thomas' poems have a religious basis. Whatever the cause of his poetic ambiguity, the result certainly ought to prevent the reader from "rushing in with the hackneyed." And yet, to these very poems, many readers have hastened in with hackneyed words such as "pagan," "pantheist," "mystic," and "religious."

"It is part of a poet's job," wrote Dylan Thomas to Pamela Hansford Johnson, "to take a debauched and prostituted word, . . . to smooth away the lines of its dissipation, and to put it on the market again, fresh and virgin."[46] Occasionally, words in the language of literary criticism become debauched by misuse and hackneyed by overwork. The aim of the discussions and examples presented in this chapter has been to create a basis for the revitalization of our terms; and perhaps it is not now entirely meaningless to say, in the phrase with which this study began, that Dylan Thomas wrote religious poetry.

[45] *Ibid.*, p. 101.
[46] "Undated, probably September 1933," *Letters*, p. 24.

**PART TWO**    The Three-Pointed Star

# Three Types of
# Religious Imagery

A basic characteristic of Thomas' poetry is a calculated ambiguity in religious matters. In the foregoing discussion of ambiguity, certain themes and images, taken as evidence of this characteristic, were subjected to a simple test. The test, which asked only whether meaning was or was not communicated readily, served to distinguish the straightforward from the ambiguous. Such a test is admittedly heavyhanded. Ignoring subtle distinctions, it presumes that all religious themes and images are of equal importance, contribute equally to the impact of the work, and operate equally in that dimension which leads us to define a poem as "religious." On the basis of that test, conclusions were uncomplicated: the presence of a religious image or theme meant something, and its absence meant something else. How these elements operated in context—whether they were functional or decorative, sincere or ironic, laudatory or condemning, serious or amusing—was not given much consideration. Nor was consideration given to a most useful distinction concerning the image itself: the distinction based on degree of Biblical denotation.

It is clear that all images and themes do not function in the same manner. For the purposes of examining Dylan Thomas' work, these functions can be differentiated into three categories. Illustrating these categories is Thomas' "Holy Spring" (p. 177), in which the following three phrases occur:

47

> . . . the spring time is all
> Gabriel and radiant shrubbery . . . ;

> My arising prodigal
> Sun the father his quiver full of the infants of
> pure fire . . . ;

> The cureless counted body . . . .

The first phrase makes reference to the Bible: Gabriel is an angel, a messenger of God, who informs Mary of her divine maternity (Luke 1:26-38) and warns Daniel of the impending destructions of war (Daniel 9:21-27). "Holy Spring" is an occasional poem concerning a springtime fire raid during World War II.[1] It makes reference to both these Biblical appearances. As the angel of the Annunciation (celebrated each spring on March 25) Gabriel comes to tell of a Saviour, amid the "radiant shrubbery" of burgeoning spring; as a prophet of destruction he comes to foretell desolation, amid the "radiant shrubbery" of a burning landscape. This poetic reference, as detailed and demanding as it is on the reader who is not completely familiar with these Biblical references, is nevertheless quite easily resolved, by a footnote or a little research, into a straightforward parallel. Operating simply as a reference to the Bible, it expands the subject, without materially altering the significance, of the poem. But it makes no further statements about whatever faith the poet may profess in the Bible or in Christianity.

In the second phrase,

> My arising prodigal
> Sun the father his quiver full of the infants of
> pure fire . . . ,

[1] Tindall, *Reader's Guide*, p. 265.

48

the specific reference is to the rising sun, seen by the poet as he climbs "Out of a bed of love" after a night of bombing. The pun of "son" on "sun" creates the allusion to the Prodigal Son (Luke 15:11-32), and identifies the sun as both a spendthrift of its bounty and a wanderer returned. "Sun the father" can be taken to describe the sun as a kind of pagan god, the central fathering creator of all things: elsewhere in the poem Thomas mentions "the god stoning night," and this particular sun-god seems an archer with rays for arrows. Again in the dimension of the pun "*son* the father" alludes to the Christian doctrine of the Trinity, and specifically to the unity of Father and Son. The image describes the poet himself, who, already a son, arises from a "bed of love" where he may well have become a father. In another dimension, the "arising prodigal / Sun the father" is also the penis, ready to produce from its "quiver" (a case for carrying arrows; or a state of quivering) the "infants of pure fire." Arrows as metaphor for children also has a specific Biblical foundation: "As arrows are in the hand of a mighty man; so are children of the youth. Happy is the man that hath his quiver full of them . . ." (Psalm 127:4-5). Hardly as uncomplicated as the direct reference to "Gabriel," this second type of image carries a multitude of meanings. Since one of these is the result of Biblical allusion, and since the many meanings within one image can never be kept entirely separate, the image as a whole reflects, to some degree, the poet's disposition towards the Scriptures. Our approach to his attitude—how we are to connect what he may intend with what he in fact says— is open to considerable interpretation. The interaction of the Biblical allusion with these meanings of sun-god, phallus, archer, and poet may be construed as irreverent

and pagan, smutty and blasphemous, vital and invigor-
ating, expansive and compendious, or merely confused.
In any case it is complex, for while it cannot be taken
as proof of a particular commitment to Christianity, it
seems to involve an attitude toward Biblical religion.

But there is a third type of imagery at work here.
The phrase "The cureless counted body," an example,
is only a partial one; for this type of imagery (more
a question of united themes than discrete images) dif-
fuses throughout the poem, contributing to the tone of
the whole. The "body" is "cureless" because, involved
in life's processes, it is ultimately subject to a dissolu-
tion that no cure can combat. The word "cure," how-
ever, refers originally to the cure of souls that was the
spiritual function of a curate, or parish priest. Although
priestless (several lines later the poet will "Call for
confessor . . . but there is none"), his body is neverthe-
less "counted." This word, appearing frequently in the
Bible with the sense of "accounted" or "judged," also
can mean "numbered," and suggests divine protection:
Job says "Doth not he see my ways, and count all my
steps?" (31:4), and Jesus affirms that "the very hairs
of your head are all numbered" (Matthew 10:30).
Thomas frequently associates the word with divine ac-
tion, as in his reference to One who "walked on the
earth in the evening / Counting the denials of the
grains" (p. 173), in which the allusion is to "the Lord
God walking in the garden in the cool of the day"
(Genesis 3:8), or in his phrase "Who'd raise the or-
gans of the counted dust" (p. 129), which alludes to
the innumerable multitude of Abram's progeny and the
phrase "if a man can number the dust of the earth,
then shall thy seed be numbered" (Genesis 13:16). The
faith expressed in the phrase "cureless counted body,"

then, is that the body, although priestless and subject to process, is under divine care. The imagery that informs the poem substantiates this idea: the vocabulary of these twenty-four lines includes "confessor," "god," "holy maker," "Praise," "blessed," "stand and sing," and "holy spring." These words establish a tone, which justifies the interpretation of "cureless counted body" as a statement about faith. This tone, restricting possible interpretations, clarifies the poet's use of the complex Prodigal Son image, which can now be taken as neither irreverence nor mere smut, but as an inclusive image that expands the limits of this poem of praise by connecting God the Creator with creative gods and pro-creative fathers.

The first of these categories, illustrated by the phrase "Gabriel and radiant shrubbery," may be called "referential imagery." Its defining characteristic is a direct and specific reference to an identifiably Biblical person or place or thing. The second type, illustrated by the "prodigal / Sun" image, may be called "allusive imagery." More complex than the first type, it alludes to Biblical religion in a way that may not be immediately obvious, and it often complicates the allusion by carrying other meanings, unrelated to religion, within its words. The third type, which was illustrated by the phrase "The cureless counted body," may be called "thematic imagery." Whatever reference or allusion is contained within such an image is of a contingent nature, depending for its support on the remaining images and themes in the work and in other works. Taken out of context, a thematic image loses much of its meaning. The phrase "cureless counted body," if found in a poem otherwise unconcerned with religious matters, would probably convey no religious meaning, whereas both "Gabriel" and "prodigal / Sun," regardless of context, direct the reader's attention to the Bible.

Referential imagery refers to the Bible. Allusive imagery, less specific, alludes to it. A word should be said here about the use of the words "reference" and "allusion." "Reference" is commonly taken to mean a specific and direct mention of something; "allusion" ordinarily means an indirect reference. In the interests of keeping these terms separate, it is best to apply "reference" to cases in which images drawn from other artistic or historical works, or from life, intrude into the work under consideration with unavoidable clarity. Such clarity, often the result of using a proper name, can arise in the absence of a name from the obvious presence of well-defined characteristics associated with that name. Clearly, the word "Christ" constitutes an unavoidable reference. But, in Thomas' poem "In the beginning" (p. 27), the line "The blood that touched the crosstree and the grail" is also an unavoidable reference, by way of the gospels and the grail legend, to the blood of Jesus. It is best to reserve "allusion" for cases in which the characteristics suggesting the unnamed thing are *not* obvious, and in which the association is not unavoidable. Such a distinction, not absolute, is related to the earlier discussion of obscurity, in that it is often determined by what the reader brings to the work. A reader totally unacquainted with the Bible might find many of Thomas' references obscure. A reader with a fair knowledge of the Biblical narratives, able to identify the references, might still find the poetry obscured by allusions. A reader willing to devote time and energy can dispel a great deal of obscurity as he uncovers the objects of Thomas' allusions. If we are willing to include, under the heading of "reference," more than just the use of proper names, and if we are willing to restrict the category of "allusion" to the less obvious incidents of indirect reference, then the terms "referential imagery" and "allusive imagery" will be more meaningful.

Thematic imagery avoids Biblical reference or allusion. This third type has something in common with allusive imagery that separates it from referential imagery, namely ambiguity. Searching a Thomas poem for religious material, the reader quickly focuses on a Biblical reference. Such a reference—the name "Adam," for example, or the word "crucifixion"—can function in a number of ways. It can be part of a firmly religious statement, or even part of an absolute denial of Biblical faith. But there is no question about its source: the presence of the Bible as an element of the poetic material is undoubtedly established. In contrast, an image that makes a religious statement by means of either an allusion or a complete avoidance of Biblical terms is an image that can remain ambiguous. Not limited to a fixed meaning and a defined set of literary or religious associations, such an image appears in several dimensions at once. As a result, it can embody complex religious statement. Drawing metaphors for religious experience from several dimensions, an image of this sort allows analogy, rather than direct ontological exposition, to define the depth and breadth of experience. Ambiguity, then, permits profundity. Religion, one of the most profound subjects of man's inquiries, often demands just this kind of expression, expression that leans more toward ambiguous profundity than concise simplification.

Since the third type of religious imagery has been named "thematic imagery," a clarification of the words "image" and "theme" is in order. This type certainly involves an image, for it consists of a clearly delineated set of words that suggest a substantive construction. Having a relevance greater than the denotative value of its words, it is the basis of metaphor.[2] In function, the substantive part of an image can rarely be separated from its immediate context. This context, which can include any part of speech, most frequently includes modifiers. The phrase "white giant's thigh," for example, is a literary image. Unless hunting grammar, the reader probably apprehends this phrase as a unit rather than thinking primarily of the substantive "thigh" and only secondarily of the modifiers "white" and "giant." In fact —since thighs are less extraordinary than white giants—he may well respond more acutely to the modifiers than to the substantive. Again, the line "The sun shipwrecked west on a pearl" ("Ballad of the Long-legged Bait," p. 166), is an image. Although "sun" is the primary substantive candidate, no benefit obtains from treating it alone as the image. The verb "shipwrecked," by itself no image, nevertheless contributes to the imagery, which, founded on the substantive "sun," pictures a ship being wrecked. "Image," then, will convey most when considered contextually. In context, it is perhaps reasonable to define image as the basis of a substantive metaphor. For an image is partly, but not exclusively, substantive; it will, however, always connote a substantive.

Unlike an image, a theme is not usually restricted to

---

[2] Although the following discussion departs slightly from Professor Unterecker's conception, I am indebted to his definition of "image" as "the substantive from which a metaphor can be constructed"; see John Unterecker, *A Reader's Guide to William Butler Yeats* (New York, 1959), p. 33.

one group of contiguous words. Like its musical counterpart, a literary theme permeates the work, reappearing, with variations, as the work progresses. And, while image suggests a concrete substantive construction (an image of judge, for example, or of garden, or pencil), theme implies either abstract substantive or verbal construction, so that we speak of the theme of justice, or of growth, or of writing. Furthermore, an image may represent one thing in one work and something quite different in another. Thomas' use of images of summer and apples, in the "boys of summer" who "drown the cargoed apples in their tides" (p. 1), is radically different from his use of the same images in "Poem in October":

> And down the other air and the blue altered sky
> Streamed again a wonder of summer
> With apples
> Pears and red currants.
>
> (p. 114)

Images, often confined to the works they inform, draw a great measure of their meaning from their immediate context. Themes, larger than the works they inform, generally have an independent significance that is, at least in part, conventional. This significance arises either from the body of literature out of which the theme is drawn or from the poet's use of that theme in his other work: "cureless counted body," for example, involves the theme of counting that gains significance from the Bible as well as from some other Thomas poems.

A thematic image, then, unites theme and image. It is a specific, discrete image that functions as a locus for one reappearance of a larger theme. Because it states the essence of an entire theme in a concise, compendious image, it is more capable of carrying the central meaning of the work than either referential or allusive imagery.

Another sort of distinction may be drawn among these three types of imagery. This distinction is based on integration. Of the three types, referential imagery is the least integrated into the work: it is often composed of one or two key words, and these words stand out as obvious Biblical references. "Gabriel," in the example from "Holy Spring," is the one word that creates the religious image. It is not so tightly woven within the skein of the other words that its removal would unravel the entire poem; in fact, it is easy to visualize another word—Samson, perhaps—replacing it. Replacing it would completely change the patent meaning of the image, to be sure; but the significance of Biblical reference in relation to the rest of the poem would be of the same order.

An allusive image sends its roots much deeper, and draws sustenance from many other words in the work. To replace either "prodigal" or "Sun," in the phrase "My arising prodigal / Sun the father his quiver full of the infants of pure fire," would be disruptive: the phrase "prodigal / Sun" is an entity. Moreover, to remove this entity would affect a number of other words. The loss of "prodigal" and its attendant notion of "spendthrift" would alter the significance of the quiver-and-arrows image, since "quiver full" implies a storing or hoarding of the arrows that are to be spent. The loss of "Sun" would affect "arising" as well as "pure fire"; and the loss of the punned "son" would affect "father" and "infants."

A thematic image is wholly integrated into the texture of the work. In fact, the integration is so complete—the image is so much a part of the entire work, and shares its statements so successfully with other statements—that, on a superficial reading, its special meaning can be missed. Were "cureless counted body" removed or replaced, other elements of the poem would help cover its loss. But, in any final analysis of the poem's statements, this phrase plays an essential—maybe *the* essential—part: for it is this one image, more than any other, that seems to convey the entire significance of "Holy Spring." For this reason, the image must be read contextually. Perhaps it is impossible to consider replacing it; but, if it be conceivable, the effect on the poem may be seen by replacing "The cureless counted body" with the line "My holy lucky body" from an earlier poem ("Unluckily for a Death," p. 120). The presence of these three spurious words in the intruded line could be rationalized: "holy" would work well in the context of the later poem, and the speaker, having escaped death in an air raid, could be considered "lucky." But the tone shifts abruptly with such a line: the conjunction of the later poem's grand "immortal hospital" and the personal, ungeneralized "My," the union of miraculously avoided death with ordinary secular luck, the pun on "wholly" which is not directly relevant to the other uses of "holy" in "Holy Spring," are but a few reasons why this replacement would have, in context, an uncomplicated and even cavalier aspect. Such an argument, completely conjectural, in no way substantiates the excellence claimed for the later poem's image; to reject the alternative is not to justify the original. However, it helps demonstrate the integrity of the original phrase. And it offers yet another characteristic of this third type of imagery: it is, in Thomas' word, inevitable. More than the other two types, thematic imagery involves words that, not appearing "chosen," have that quality of "strong, inevitable pulling" that Thomas made a requirement of good poetry.[3]

With these two criteria of (1) degree of Biblical denotation and (2) degree of integration into the poem, the religious images found in Thomas' poetry may be more readily discussed. By distinguishing among these types, rather than by grouping all phrases that invoke Biblical reference into one vast catalogue, some of the subtlety of Thomas' poetic method can be better appreciated, and some of his more serious statements about religious matters can be precipitated out of the great pool of his religious imagery. To get the requisite tools of analysis firmly in hand, then, a study of each type of religious imagery is in order.[4]

[3] See above, pp. 33-34.

[4] At this point, two qualifications of this method had best be offered. Like any application of categories to literature, this method is approximate. Since there is no absolute boundary between reference and allusion, there can be no absolute boundary between the first and second types of imagery; and numerous examples will be found that can, with justification, be included in either group. Similarly, since a veiled allusion to a ubiquitous Biblical image can resemble a general reference to a widespread Biblical theme, the boundary between the second and third types will occasionally be obscured. Hopefully, the usefulness of this method will outweigh these disadvantages.

Secondly, these three types do not claim to be exhaustive. While it seems probable that no other significant categories can be found, this three-part division is not offered as "*the* three types" but simply as "three types."

To begin, then, with Adam. In "Fern Hill" (pp. 178-180) Adam is a figure of innocence. The narrator, a boy "young and easy" and "carefree," awakens from dreams to discover that the farm has once again come back to his consciousness: ". . . it was all / Shining, it was Adam and maiden." Although it is the only referential religious image in the poem, this phrase is sufficient to establish the Biblical parallel. It brings into focus the lines immediately following ("The sky gathered again / And the sun grew round that very day"): Creation is repeated in this suggestion of Genesis. Thomas often expresses growing up or waking up in imagery drawn from the first chapter of Genesis: growing awareness is indicated by the increasing differentiation of an originally uniform world.[1] The reference to Adam also establishes the subsequent lines ("So it must have been after the birth of the simple light / In the first, spinning place . . .") as an allusion to the paradise of the Garden of Eden. It is noteworthy, in this image of "Adam and maiden," that "maiden" implies "virgin"; the Fall, associated with sexual experience, has not yet disturbed this paradise, as it has not yet disturbed the boy in the poem. Adam, metaphor for original innocence, causes no confusion of meaning and implies no confession of faith.

Nor is there any confusion about the Adam images in

---

[1] This use of imagery is examined further in the discussion of Thomas' story "The Tree"; see Appendix.

"Ceremony After a Fire Raid" (pp. 143-146). Here, however, paradise is not simply innocent. Sacrificial aspects of the Creation and Fall are also considered. Adam and Eve, along with "bullock," "lamb," and "virgin," represent victims that have been killed with "A child of a few hours" in the raid.

> I know not whether
> Adam or Eve, the adorned holy bullock
> Or the white ewe lamb
> Or the chosen virgin
> Laid in her snow
> On the altar of London
> Was the first to die
> In the cinder of the little skull.

In these lines the syntax, far from simple, establishes that Adam, Eve, and child are the three subjects under consideration: the "adorned holy bullock" is in apposition with "Adam," the "white ewe lamb" is in apposition with "Eve," and the "chosen virgin" is the child. Adam, Eve, and child seem contemporaries. Which of them was "the first to die" in the child's mind—whether the original victims of the Creation or the child herself first felt death—is not known. Nor is it known whether the child, at the instant of her death, lost her faith in the story of Adam and Eve. The narrator does know, however, that

> . . . the legend
> Of Adam and Eve is never for a second
> Silent in my service.

The "service" here is the poet's own performance of worship; it is also his servitude both to the Deity and to the process of life and death that is imaged by Adam and Eve. Related to his own life, the original Creation is also related to this child's death; for the Fall of Adam and Eve from their innocence implies the possibility of innocent death for a child such as this. Their legend is never silent, although Adam and Eve, "bride and bride groom," are

> Lying in the lull
> Under the sad breast of the head stone
> White as the skeleton
> Of the garden of Eden.

What is said in this passage about Adam and Eve and their garden is straightforward: the garden of Eden is only a skeleton, an apparition of a paradise that is no longer a relevant metaphor for this postdiluvian world. Adam and Eve, "Lying in the lull," are buried in the calm after death; they also, perhaps, dissimulate the truth with their legends of Edenic innocence.

Unlike allusive images, these referential images do not combine many meanings into their few words. A referential image rarely carries, within itself, a poetic comment on the image. It cannot; there is no room, within the substantive words that form the reference, for such a comment, unless the substantive is split open by a pun on a name. Such a pun can occur: the phrase "God's Mary in her grief" (p. 84), if heard as "God's *merry* in her grief," qualifies the image of Mary (Mary is merry) as well as the image of God (God is not only merry, but Mary; or, God delights to see Mary's grief). However, most referential images suggest without question a Biblical person, place, or thing, and a conventional interpretation of that person, place, or thing.

Referential images, unable to carry secondary, qualifying meanings within themselves, may nevertheless be qualified immediately by context. In "Altarwise by owl-light" Adam is the subject of some joking. Sonnet III speaks of "Adam's wether in the flock of horns, / Butt of the tree-tailed worm that mounted Eve" (p. 81). Adam, here, is the butt of the joke. Cuckolded by the worm, he is a wether (a castrated ram), which, sexually impotent, wears cuckold's horns on its head for butting. Later in the poem (Sonnet VI) Adam is referred to as "time's joker." As joker he becomes "bell-voiced Adam" (Sonnet VII) because of the bells worn on a jester's costume; the reference is also to the *bell-wether*, which is a leader of sheep as Adam is a leader —the original, in fact—of cuckolds. These phrases demand a knowledge of the story of Eve and the serpent; they also demand a fanciful extension of that story. The notion of Adam as cuckold is an interpretation introduced by Thomas. Image, here, is one thing; what Thomas says *about* the image is quite another.

In the above examples of referential imagery, the figure of Adam demands two different metaphoric interpretations. Because of the association with Eden, he is a representative of paradisical innocence; because of his betrayal by Eve and serpent, and his subsequent Fall, he is a type of victim sacrificed either to death or to humor. Both of these uses depend, for their success, on the reader's knowledge of the Biblical story of Adam and Eve. This dependence is of a primary importance. Since no pun lurks in these uses of the word "Adam," a suggestion of the story of Genesis is the primary function of the image. Once the reference is comprehended, no further effort at interpretation is required of the reader; Thomas may tell something more about the image, but the image itself has done all it can do.

Clearly, such an image makes no particular personal religious statement. To see the phrase

> I know the legend
> Of Adam and Eve is never for a second
> Silent in my service

as a statement of religious commitment is to overstate the force of a referential image. It demands no faith for a poet to appeal to "the legend / Of Adam and Eve"; by itself, the presence of this legend in a poem is proof of nothing except the poet's acquaintance with the Biblical story of the garden of Eden. And it is precisely because such a confusion can and does arise— because, that is, images such as these are taken as evidence of Thomas' religious conviction—that a distinction among types of imagery is necessary. The statements made by means of allusive and thematic images can, and often do, reveal Thomas' relationship to his religious material; those made by referential images, unless they are substantiated by other statements, simply refer.

Like the story of Genesis, the story of Samson (Judges 13-16) provides Thomas with imagery. There is an excellent example of a simple referential image in "Into her Lying Down Head" (pp. 125-127), a poem concerning the poet's wife and her faithless dreams. Complaining of the wife's betrayal with "A furnace-nostrilled column-membered / Super-or-near man"—the fabulous sexual paragon she encounters in her dreams —the poet catalogues the masochistic images of lust that are his "enemies":

> Juan aflame and savagely young King Lear,
> Queen Catherine howling bare
> And Samson drowned in his hair.

*63*

Samson, a hero of colossal strength whose somewhat weaker morals led him into meretricious relationships with various women, came to his ultimate downfall as a result of betrayal by Delilah. In this poem the image suggests two aspects of the Samson story. The primary aspect is that of strength: since the secret of Samson's strength lies in his uncut hair, a Samson "drowned in his hair" is (if "drowned" is taken figuratively) a Samson adorned in a profusion of hair, and hence strong and lusty. Another meaning, of secondary importance because "drowned" is not an accurate description of Samson's manner of death, nevertheless makes a tangential connection to the idea of betrayal that runs throughout the poem. The suggestion of betrayal depends on the more literal meaning of "drowned" as "killed." It is the very existence of his hair that makes possible Samson's betrayal and ultimate death: "drowned in his hair," he is killed by it. But, like Don Juan, Queen Catherine, and a hypothetically young King Lear, Samson here suggests primarily a powerful lover. Religion plays little part in the selection of this image; the fact that it is taken from the Bible does not significantly modify the meaning of the poem.

In a similar way, the religious nature of a Samson figure in "How shall my animal" (pp. 100-101) is of small consequence. Although the name "Samson" does not appear, the suggestions given make the reference unavoidable. The passage in question, with the key words italicized, follows:

> Sigh long, clay cold, lie *shorn,*
> Cast high, stunned on gilled stone; *sly scissors*
> *ground in frost*
> *Clack through the thicket of strength, love*
> *hewn in pillars drops*

With carved bird, saint, and sun, the wrack-
   spiked *maiden mouth*
*Lops*, as a bush plumed with flames, *the rant*
   *of the fierce eye,*
*Clips short the gesture of breath.*

Samson is "shorn" of his locks by the "sly" scissors of a
deceitful Delilah, whose love, hardly honest, was cold as
"frost." He causes his own death by pushing apart the
"hewn . . . pillars" of his captors' palace. Before death
he has been blinded: the wily "maiden mouth," coaxing
out his secret, is responsible for lopping "the rant of
the fierce eye," and for "clipping" short his life. Sam-
son's life—a life of strength and final betrayal as a result
of inherent weakness—is simply a metaphor for the life
of the poet's "animal," which is itself a metaphor for the
creative imagination. And these metaphors have no
particular religious significance.

In the poem " 'If my head hurt a hair's foot' " (pp.
108-109) the mother answers the unborn child's
speeches with the words

"No. Not for Christ's dazzling bed
   Or a nacreous sleep among soft particles
   and charms
   My dear would I change my tears or
   your iron head."

Christ, here, serves as an image of a glorious martyr.
Since childbirth, intimately connected with beds, is
the subject of the poem, an earlier phrase, "The bed is
a cross place," might be relevant to this reference.
Brought to bed with child, mother martyrs herself and
experiences pain that another may live. In any case,
"Christ's dazzling bed" remains a simple comparison
that implies no deeper religious meaning.

"Vision and Prayer" (pp. 154-165), a fundamentally religious work, contains an image that can be distinguished, by its simplicity, from the major statements of the poem. In Part II, death is described as "forever falling night," and those who die are actively falling as they travel through eternity. As travellers, they chart and follow a course. Stanza 4, Part II, contains the following image:

> Now common lazarus
> Of the charting sleepers prays
> Never to awake and arise.

Contented with death, this "common lazarus," representative of all the resurrectable dead, prefers his unresurrected sleep. Comprehension of this image involves only a knowledge of the story (John 11:1-45) of Jesus raising Lazarus from the grave.

"Ballad of the Long-legged Bait" (pp. 166-176), in describing the whales that chase the bait, contains the line "O, Jericho was falling in their lungs!" (p. 168). Jericho was captured by Joshua (Joshua 6), whose forces, trumpeting and shouting, roared its walls to the ground. These whales, like Joshua's people, are noisy and destructive. They are not, however, religious. Neither are Susannah and Sheba, who appear later in the poem: "Sussanah's drowned in the bearded stream / And no-one stirs at Sheba's side" (p. 171). These women, part of a catalogue that includes "Venus," and personified Sin with "a woman's shape," and some "Masthigh moon-white women naked," are the stuff of erotic dreams, shown by a "tempter under the eyelid." As such, they are simply examples of lovely, desirable females; their religious associations are distinctly irrelevant.

From this examination of referential images, some conclusions can be drawn about how they function and what they contribute to a work. In such images, Thomas treats the Bible not as a basis for religion but as a body of mythology.[2] It becomes a storehouse of well-known symbols and tales into which he dips from time to time. The images he draws strengthen his writings by their appeal to an accepted and reverenced standard; they do not imply that he is living under the authority of that standard. Operating as metaphors that link his individual poetic embodiments with their archetypes, they bring the archetype into the frame of reference for the purpose of comparison. No question of faith is raised. The reader is not asked, in the presence of such images, either to sympathize with Biblical religion or willingly to suspend his disbelief any more than, in the presence of the phrase "And that's the rub" (p. 14), he is asked to put his faith in *Hamlet*, or, in the presence of the line "Venus lies star-struck in her wound" (p. 171), he is asked to sympathize with classical mythology. Were questions of Biblical faith important, the reader of "Ballad of the Long-legged Bait" would have to insist on drawing a distinction between canonical Sheba and apocryphal Susannah; in fact, however, the one source of legend is as good as the other in the realm of referential imagery.

But the very fact that a referential image is Biblical (as opposed, that is, to Homeric or Shakespearean) can profoundly affect a poem, in that it can lead the reader to interpret other passages of the poem in Biblical terms. Such is the case in "Fern Hill," where the single

---

[2] Mythology, in this sense, is "the use of symbols which is not bound up with belief in its symbols" (D. G. James, *Scepticism and Poetry*, p. 245).

image of Adam brings the lines following it into order. There is a danger in such interpretation, however: a reader may begin to assume that every Biblical image evinces a deep religious conviction. The use of a number of Biblical images can produce an atmosphere infused with apparent religious significance yet devoid of any real comprehensible statements about the poet's religion; and in Thomas' work, direct Biblical reference is frequently unrelated to statements of commitment. It is true that referential religious imagery necessarily brings the matter of religion into a poem in the clearest, most obvious, manner. But the obvious is sometimes the shallow. Recognizing referential imagery as a distinct and limited type, the reader is better prepared to contemplate the obvious without becoming the dupe of the superficial.

While referential imagery reveals, allusive imagery both reveals and conceals. Of a referential image one question must always be asked: why is the reader's attention being directed to Biblical religion? Of an allusive image there are always two questions to ask: why is Biblical religion being presented to the reader, and, why is Biblical religion simultaneously being disguised or masked? For allusive imagery is characterized by disguise, and any disguise or mask both reveals the fundamental form and conceals the specific detail of the wearer's features. As a result, disguise establishes a kind of tension within the figure, a tension between the patent outward appearance and the suspected underlying reality. This tension creates, between figure and mask, a dynamic relationship in which mask continually comments on figure and figure continually comments on mask.

Drama, depending on disguise, provides examples of this relationship. A play that comments upon the nature of this disguise—*A Midsummer Night's Dream*—provides an excellent one in Snug, the joiner dressed as the lion. It is the function of Snug, as lion, to suggest fear, while lion, as mere Snug, elicits laughter. Both the character of Snug and the character of lion are altered by this disguise. And Bottom, speaking better than he knows—although not better than Shakespeare the author knows, for whom Bottom the character is a disguise—insists on the interrelationship when he says: "Nay, you must name his name, and half his face must be seen through the lion's neck, and he himself must speak through saying thus. . . . 'If you think I come hither as a lion, it were pity of my life. No! I am no such thing. I am a man as other men are.' And there, indeed, let him name his name and tell them plainly he is Snug the joiner."[1] Bottom affirms that disguises must both reveal and conceal. But, confused about appearance and reality, he identifies Snug as "a man as other men are." The point of the disguise, however, is that Snug is *not* "a man as other men are," but something different. Snug as man, and lion as animal, each pursues a single existence, and functions within the realm of that existence. Snug as lion, however, must function simultaneously within each realm; his every action, of necessity a manly action, must be consonant with lionliness. Since both realms inhere in each of his acts, each realm will effect a difference in the other.

This difference, created in the figure by the mask and in the mask by the figure, is the essential feature of allusive imagery. Just as it is not enough to say of Snug that he is a man like other men, so it is not enough to say of an allusive image that it is a Biblical reference like other Biblical references. Nor is it enough, ignoring the man and seeing only the pelt, to write off the Biblical reference as unimportant and treat the contextual meaning of the image as the only relevant meaning. The tension created by this difference allows a poem to comment on the religious image while the image is commenting on the poem. In this way, an allusive image carries reference as well as an attitude towards that reference.

In imagery, as in drama, a disguise requires neither an absence of nor a complete change of name. Naming

[1] *A Midsummer Night's Dream*, iii, i, 37-47.

a Biblical figure does not automatically create refer-
ential rather than allusive imagery. If the name, in its
context, insists on a meaning other than a conventional
one, a disguise is present: the meaning of one word has
borrowed the clothing of another. The simplest exam-
ple is probably the phrase "Jacob to the stars" ("Altar-
wise by owl-light," p. 80), in which "Jacob," no longer
the Biblical noun, is a verb meaning something like
"build a Jacob's ladder." Not simply a one-for-one cor-
respondence of meanings, however, this trope also
seems to include, in context, the sense of "wrestle"
(since Jacob wrestled with an angel), and "masturbate"
(punning on the vulgar "jack off"). These several senses,
reacting with one another, produce an overall meaning
that is certainly not simply that of the Biblical name.

Further examples of allusive imagery will help clarify
this notion of disguise. "Adam," as was noted, is fre-
quently a referential image. In several of Thomas'
early poems, however, the word becomes surrogate for
another meaning, a meaning revealed in the seven-
stanza poem "I dreamed my genesis" (pp. 33-34). This
poem presents two dreams. The initial one, contained
in the first three stanzas, concerns the narrator's con-
ception and prenatal existence.

> I dreamed my genesis in sweat of sleep,
>    breaking
> Through the rotating shell, strong
> As motor muscle on the drill . . . .

His "genesis" is sexual: "shell" seems mother, and
"motor muscle," father. In these stanzas the poet's gen-
esis is depicted in images that partly conceal the sexual
interpretation. In the next three stanzas, which describe
another dream beginning "I dreamed my genesis and

71

died again," the imagery is more patently sexual. Images of violent death and resurrection replace those of conception and birth, and this sexual dream ends with erection and emission:

> And power was contagious in my birth, second
> Rise of the skeleton and
> Rerobing of the naked ghost. Manhood
> Spat up from the resuffered pain.

The seventh and final stanza summarizes these dreams of genesis; the poet affirms that he has

> ... fallen
> Twice in the feeding sea, grown
> Stale of Adam's brine . . . .

Exhausted by his dreams, he has no more use for "Adam's brine," which is both the product of his emission and the amniotic sea of his genesis. His erection, the cause of genesis, ends, like Adam, in a fall. Thomas, linking genesis and sex, moves from genesis to Genesis, and Adam is established as a surrogate for phallus.[2]

---

[2] Whether or not Thomas actually recorded two of his dreams in this poem is unknown; in any case this pattern, of a disguised sexual dream followed by a second more obvious sexual dream ending in emission, is noted by Freud as a common one (Sigmund Freud, *The Interpretation of Dreams*, trans. James Strachey [New York, 1965], Ch. 4, section C, p. 370). Eighteen years after the publication of this poem, Thomas, responding to a question about the influence of Freud on his poetry, replied: "I have read only one book of Freud's, 'The Interpretation of Dreams,' and do not recall having been influenced by it in any way" ("Poetic Manifesto," p. 50). It seems more probable that the sequence recorded in this poem was drawn from Thomas' experience than that it was fashioned from his imagination in accordance with Freudian principles.

Adam as phallus clarifies several other poems. "My world is pyramid" (pp. 35-37), which immediately follows "I dreamed my genesis," begins with a similar Adam image and a mechanical description of intercourse: "Half of the fellow father as he doubles / His sea-sucked Adam in the hollow hulk." In "When, like a running grave" (pp. 21-23), the image is qualified: "Joy is the knock of dust, Cadaver's shoot / Of bud of Adam through his boxy shift." The "joy" here is sexual. "Cadaver's shoot" comes from the "bud of Adam." It is the emission that, since it creates life, also creates eventual death and the promise of burial in the "boxy shift" of the coffin—or, keeping Thomas' predilection for puns and slang in mind, in the "boxy shift" of boxer shorts or of the vagina. Buds precede flowers, and flowers are a plant's sexual organs. Adam's bud is once again the phallus that causes genesis.[3] In these images Adam is named. Double meanings abound, however, and the identity of Adam and phallus suggests further identities of Biblical Creation with sexual activity. Also suggested is the idea of contemporaneity: God's original Creation, continually repeating itself in the present, makes the story of Genesis, for Thomas, less an historical fable than a paradigm for his own particular experience.

Considering his interest in the story of the Creation, it is not surprising that a number of Thomas' images allude, namelessly, to Adam, Eve, and other elements in the first chapters of Genesis. The poem "In the beginning" (pp. 27-28), titled by the first words of the Bible, ends with "the ribbed original of love." A "three-pointed star" and a "bough of bone across the rooting air" have

[3] See Sonnet v of "Altarwise by owl-light" and stanza vi of "Vision and Prayer" for similar uses of this image.

73

already appeared.[4] This rib, with its suggestive shape, is yet another metaphor for the masculine originator of sex. It can be taken as a reference to Adam, who was "ribbed" (in the sense of "fileted" or "boned") to produce Eve. As the origin of Eve, he originated, or invented, love; but—if we are to believe the version of this tale that appears in "Altarwise by owl-light"—his love was betrayed to cuckoldry by the serpent, and Adam, original butt of a huge joke, took a ribbing. Having about it a calculated ambiguity, this line can also refer to Eve, who was both formed from Adam's rib and "ribbed" (as in "speared") by phallic rib.

Birth is also Creation in "When once the twilight locks no longer" (pp. 4-5):

> When the galactic sea was sucked
> And all the dry seabed unlocked,
> I sent my creature scouting on the globe,
> That globe itself of hair and bone
> That, sewn to me by nerve and brain,
> Had stringed my flask of matter to his rib.

When the lactic (milky) sea of the breast was exhausted and the "creature" of the self weaned, he began exploring; or, when the original waters of the earth (of galaxial proportions) were sucked down and gathered together into one place so that dry land appeared (Genesis 1:9), he, like Noah (Genesis 8:6-8), sent out a birdlike "creature" as a scout; or, when the amniotic sea was sucked out through the open locks of the womb, he was born. Genesis, metaphor for birth, continues in the last line of this stanza. An embryonic "I" is "stringed"

[4] The "three-pointed star," suggesting the Trinity, perhaps suggests sexuality as well; the number three, according to Freud, "has been confirmed from many sides as a symbol of the male genitals" (*The Interpretation of Dreams*, p. 393).

by umbilicus to mother. Since embryo is composed of mother's stuff, "flask of matter" may be "flask of *mater*." And since mother and Genesis are relevant, Eve as everywoman and as "rib" seems to be part of this reference.

Also related to Genesis are images of pavement. For Thomas the word appears to have a religious significance, and to be associated with rebirth: in "Ceremony After a Fire Raid" the burning landscape is apotheosized into "golden pavements laid in requiems" (p. 145). Pavements cover ground, and ground, sometimes walked upon by the living, more often (for Thomas) covers the dead. Rebirth involves a return through the ground: the shades of the dead, in their casket submarines, "periscope through flowers to the sky" (p. 5); and cadavers, food for roots, are botanically reincarnated as "groundworks thrusting through a pavement" (p. 81). The "tree-tailed worm that mounted Eve" and mocked Adam also did his work "On thunderous pavements" (p. 81). These uses of pavement, suggesting a connection with apotheosis, rebirth, and Eden, are all relevant to Thomas' use of "macadam," an asphalt paving material, as an image. "When, like a running grave" (pp. 21-23) contains "city tar and subway bored to foster / Man through macadam." This "macadam," literally "son of Adam," includes all men. And if man is fostered "through macadam," he will be thrust up in rebirth through this pavement from the subway below. But, since Adam-as-phallus appears three lines later (the "bud of Adam"), the "subway" that is "bored" may be sexual. The word "macadam" seems an elaborate metaphor for the process of birth (caused by "Adam") ending in death (leading to interment under pavements).

More clearly definable is an allusive image in "A grief ago": "And she who lies / Like exodus a chapter from the garden" (p. 63). Just as Exodus is a book away from Genesis, so Adam and Eve's exodus from the garden leaves them "a chapter" away from it. Eve, brought to bed with four children, does her lying in the fourth chapter of Genesis after being driven from Eden in chapter three. The woman, here, is "She who was who I hold," the narrator's partner in sex. As desirable as Eve, she is as lovely as "a chapter from the garden," a piece of beauty straight out of paradise. Here again the image, more than a comparison, suggests a real contemporaneity, an identity of former Eden with present garden.[5]

"If I were tickled by the rub of love" (pp. 13-15) includes the lines "I would not fear the apple nor the flood / Nor the bad blood of spring." To treat these three images simply as referential images—to observe only that he would not fear the original sin offered by the serpent in Eden, nor the punishment visited on antediluvian society, nor the revenge for Good Friday —is to ignore their integration into the poem. The "bad blood of spring" is the blood of birth, the "red tickle as the cattle calve" mentioned in the first stanza; it is

[5] From its context, this meditation appears to be set in a garden more local and accessible than Eden's. Evoked by images of its contents, this garden includes "flowers," "thorn," "Rose," "bud," "leaf," "seed," and a "lily's anger"; a "frog" and a "chrysalis" live among the vegetation; weird hybrids of sundial and weathervane ornament the scene ("twelve triangles of the cherub wind / Engraving going" and "suncock") as well as a "paddler's bowl" (birdbath) and a "masted venus," which is both a statuette in the birdbath and, according to Elder Olson, a name for wild teasel (*The Poetry of Dylan Thomas* [Chicago, 1954], p. 99).

also the blood roused in that season when this young man's fancy turns to love. Sex is the subject of this poem; but, says the narrator, as long as love is present I would fear neither the retributions promised in Biblical warnings nor the birth consequent upon sexual relations. The "apple," fruit of the tree, is a metaphor for child, fruit of the womb; for child is certainly fruit. "Shall it be male or female? say the cells, / And drop the plum like fire from the flesh." Fearless of the fruit, he would also take no heed of fruitlessness: "The sea of scums could drown me as it broke / Dead on the sweetheart's toes." A vulgarism for "semen," "scums" figures here in an image of onanism and sterility. Apple, flood, and blood, all basically Biblical, are here primarily obstetrical.

The poem "Where once the waters of your face" (p. 12) stretches a conceit to include at least four possible meanings. Constant throughout these, "waters of your face" remains an allusion to the "face of the waters" (Genesis 1:2) out of which the dry land appeared. The poem, as Olson interprets it, is addressed to "a dried sea channel."[6] Everything in the poem fits this interpretation: the wind blows where the water once flowed, children play on the stones among the dried weeds, coral formations cling to the bottom, and the "waters of your face" describes the former surface of the filled channel. Secondly, the poem is about birth and mother: the tears of your eyes once "Spun to my screws," says the narrator, recalling the effect of his prenatal gymnastics within the walls of the womb. Where once the fathering "mermen" entered among the "roe," a "dry wind steers," bringing (for steers are impotent) sterility. In the second stanza, the "green

[6] *Ibid.*, p. 46.

unraveller" with "scissors oiled"—the midwife—cut the "knots" of the "tied cord" and delivered the child. Like a barren Sarah, left dry and old with the "clocking tides" of her productive years "Invisible," the mother will nevertheless have by "magic" the sexual experience implied in the phrase "serpents in your tides." Thirdly, the poem describes a girl, once loved by the narrator and now only a memory. The "green knots" that "sank their splice / Into the tided cord" describes her hymenal state, green with inexperience; his "green unraveller" however, "cut the channels at their source / And lay the wet fruits low." Although his "weed of love" is now separated from her "lovebeds of the weeds," the serpents will return. The fourth interpretation, varying the above, refers not to a lover merely remembered but to a lover "dry" after consummation and soon to revive. In each of these explanations, "the waters of your face" takes on a slightly different meaning. It is the surface of ocean water, the tears of pain, the tears of joy, or, finally, the fluids of sex: for Thomas, not the first to find a sexual meaning in "face," may have recalled the perfect *double entendre* of Lear's lines "Behold yond simp'ring dame, / Whose face between her forks presageth snow" (*King Lear*, IV, vi, 120-121). Throughout these variations the Biblical reference remains to express a common denominator of all sorts of creation, procreation, and recreation.

In "Incarnative devil" (p. 46) there is a "talking snake" in a garden at "shaping-time" who "In shapes of sin forked out the bearded apple." This apple, the forbidden fruit, is served up ("forked out") by the serpent. But, like Shakespeare's "face between her forks," the fruit forked here may also be a metaphor for female genitals. The apple, "bearded" because "to beard" means "to equip with barbs," is barbed to hook the innocent Eve; and Eve is sufficiently "bearded"—taunted and tempted—by the proffered fruit.

Two additional examples of allusive imagery based on the Creation help demonstrate Thomas' continued concern with that Old Testament story. Genesis again provides metaphors for awakening in "When I woke" (pp. 150-151). Referring once more to the Creation and "the face of the waters," the poet says:

> Every morning I make,
> God in bed, good and bad,
> After a water-face walk.

Literally, the awakened narrator makes a "water-face walk" (so urgent that the need distorts his face?) to his water-closet; or, perhaps, he merely gets up to wash his face. Back in bed as "God," he recreates good and evil: for after the face of the waters are altered, Eden and its tree of the knowledge of good and evil were established. Creation's contemporary, he does for his little world what God did for His. In "Light breaks where no sun shines" (pp. 29-30), the title phrase refers, in its context, to two antipodal places: the tomb, with its luminescence of putrefaction, and the womb, with its illumination of foreknowledge. But it also alludes to the first chapter of Genesis, where, as Thomas perhaps knew, God said "Let there be light" thirteen verses before He made the sun.

In the above examples, allusive images disguise the Creation story either by suggesting it as one dimension in the ambiguity of allusion, or by transmuting it into something else under the guise of the word "Adam." Insofar as it is possible to define the function of these images, it may be said that, while referential images bring fixed and ascertainable meanings based on their Biblical existence, these allusive images project many meanings; for, blending the Biblical with the sexual, the obstetrical, the anatomical, and even the comical, these images of the Creation attain a functional complexity. This complexity, in the first place, establishes Genesis as the archetype of all sorts of creation and evolves a language that expresses the specific of birth in terms of the archetypal Creation; secondly, it compresses (as all such archetypal language does) its cosmos into a contemporaneity in which Adam and poet can coexist.

One of the clearest examples, however, of Thomas' use of religious imagery is found in his use of "Samson." "Samson," like "Adam," figures as both a referential and an allusive image. The poem "Deaths and Entrances" (pp. 129-130), another of Thomas' descriptions of a wartime fire raid, ends with the lines "Until that one loved least / Looms the last Samson of your zodiac." Several earlier phrases prefigure this image: "lions and fires," a conjunction of words that is of uncertain significance in the context of the poem, suggests the lion slain by Samson (Judges 14:5-6) and the fires he set in revenge against the Philistines (Judges 15:4-5). And the word "lock"—suggesting, among other things, locks of hair—appears several times in this poem. These suggestions, taken together with the named reference to Samson, help clarify the poem; but to know that Samson was strong and lusty is not to understand "Deaths and Entrances." "Samson" seems surrogate for another. Olson, in fact, defines "Samson of your zodiac" as "The enemy airman who will bomb London and bring down the heavens upon it as Samson overthrew the temple."[7] Samson, enemy of many, here seems to be

[7] *Ibid.*, p. 100.

an image (the "one loved least") of general enmity, a hero of such fabulous strength that, like a classical god, he is assigned to a zodiacal constellation. This image is another that borders the referential and the allusive. Not so plain that the facts of the Biblical narrative resolve it, the image seems to make one name (Samson) equivalent to another word (enemy) associated with it, as "Adam" was equated with "phallus." But, similar to the "bud of Adam" image above, it is not purely allusive. The simple replacement of "Samson" by "enemy" does not convey the entire primary meaning of the poem, since a particular Biblical reference—to one who comes from another country and topples towers in widespread and maybe self-righteous destruction—is essential.

Of a more obviously allusive nature is the Samson image from "I make this in a warring absence" (pp. 87-89). The relevant lines are

> I make a weapon of an ass's skeleton
> And walk the warring sands by the dead town,
> Cudgel great air, wreck east, and topple
>     sundown,
>
> . . . . . . . . . . . . . . . . . . . . . . . . . . . . .
>
> Destruction, picked by birds, brays through
>     the jawbone,

and, from two later stanzas, "The hero's head lies scraped of every legend" and "These once-blind eyes have breathed a wind of vision." The first passage quoted above, a magnificent description of raging destructive impulses occasioned by a lovers' quarrel, suggests, by "ass's skeleton" and "jaw-bone," the "new jawbone of an ass" (Judges 15:15) with which Samson slew a thousand Philistines. Once again the conjunction of love and destruction is imaged by Samson. Here, however, another element resides. Conscious of the poet's task—"this," in the title, refers to the poem he makes—the narrator saves himself, by a modicum of self-awareness, from the stultification inherent in his anger. It is the poetry of destruction—his own poetry— that "brays through the jaw-bone" of this roaring and somewhat asinine figure. The scraped head and the "once-blind eyes" further connect the figure with Samson: shaved in betrayal by Delilah, Samson was then blinded. In context, these two latter lines refer specifically to aspects of death and resurrection which, according to Thomas, are the themes of their stanzas.[8] They only suggest Samson by virtue of the earlier appearance of the jawbone image. Samson, then, figures in this poem; but so does a particular attitude towards him. He is depicted here as something of a fool and something of a noisy belligerent who, finding a weapon, made himself an ass.[9]

A brilliant compression of this same image appears in "All all and all the dry worlds lever" (pp. 38-39): "Man of my flesh, the jawbone riven, / Know now the flesh's lock and vice." Seeing himself as an equivalent of a Philistine, or one who has been riven by Samson's flailing jawbone, the poet tells himself of the flesh's weaknesses that, in Samson's case, are his undoing: the "lock" of hair and the "vice" of venery that will lead his enemy to the mechanical "lock and vice" of the "fetters of brass" (Judges 16:21) with which he was bound. Sam-

---

[8] Letter to Hermann Peschmann, "1st February 1938," *Letters*, pp. 185-186.

[9] Likewise, Thomas characterized the hypocrisy and pompous rhetoric of Ann's mourners in "After the funeral" (p. 96) with the words "mule praises, brays."

son, as enemy, is metaphor for fleshly vices. This image also includes "jawbone" as metaphor for poetic tool: for Thomas, who said "Man be my metaphor" (p. 15), saw in the process of poetic creation a process by which man was hewn, or "riven," out of language.

"In the white giant's thigh" (pp. 197-199) includes, in the phrase "torch of foxes" (p. 198), a perfect example of allusive imagery. Biblical background helps here. Samson, attracted by a Philistine woman, had gone to her country to marry her (Judges 14). Having slain a lion on his way, and having later discovered a bees' nest and honey in the abandoned carcass, he had posed a riddle to the guests at the wedding feast, the answer to which involved lion and honey. His wife, in collusion with the guests, let out the answer, and Samson accused her of faithlessness. She was given, consequently, to another, and Samson, enraged at his father-in-law, turned incendiary and fired the latter's wheatfields by tying torches to foxes' tails and driving them through the standing crops.

The narrator of this poem, hardly an arsonist, evokes memories of the long-dead women lying in graves on "the high chalk hill" beneath his feet. Echoes of the Samson story sound throughout the poem. The women, "a bloom of wayside brides in the hawed house," are surrounded by images of marriage festivity: "their clogs danced in the spring," and there are "rush / Lights" (torches) around to light up the viands prepared in the "ox roasting sun."[10] Although foxes are the nearest here

---

[10] Also a possible allusion to the *Odyssey*, Book XII, "ox roasting sun" suggests the roasting of the Oxen of the Sun by Ulysses' mariners. Paralleling the incontinence of Thomas' girls, their action, also proscribed, was likewise urgent, enjoyable, and apparently essential to survival.

to Samson's lion, these long-gone girls had "breasts full
of honey." And, as careless about their loyalties as Sam-
son's wife was of hers—"If ye had not plowed with my
heifer," hints Samson darkly to the guests, "ye had
not found out my riddle" (Judges 14:18)—Thomas'
girls enjoyed their promiscuity, and ". . . gay with any
one / Young as they in the after milking moonlight
lay." Living, like the Philistines, in their rural society,
the women hear the "lewd, wooed fields" around them;
it is in this countryside that "a torch of foxes foams"
and where "All birds and beasts in the linked night
uproar and chime." The word "linked" means, plainly,
coupled: the night is alive with sexual activity. But
"link" is also a word meaning both "torch" and "lax in
respect to religious observances." Fiery, sexual Samson
was "link" in this respect; so, probably, were the girls.
The poem, however, is not. A number of words suggest
worship. These are perhaps intended to suggest the
Bible, and thereby to give support to the Samson al-
lusion; the vocabulary includes "pray," "friars," "aisles,"
"crossed / Their breast," "kneels," "bell," "Sundays,"
"lighted shapes of faith" (heavenly bodies or church
windows?) and "grass gulfed cross" (overgrown grave
marker).

Near the end of the poem the foxes reappear, in "fox
cubbed / Streets" and in the final line: "And the daugh-
ters of darkness flame like Fawkes fires still." "Fawkes
fires" are the effigies or bonfires burnt on Guy Fawkes
Day; like Guy Fawkes, an unsuccessful pyrophile, Sam-
son (a successful one) and these women are remem-
bered with fires. But these fires, more than bonfires, are
foxfire; foxfire, an eerie luminescence seen in decaying
wood, is suggested by the "crumbled wood" three lines
from the end and by the fact that the earlier "torch of

foxes" was located "Quick in the wood." This image, not only recalling a November holiday, describes the slow and smoldering decomposition of these women.

Fire and foxes, then, are connected here as securely as they were by the crafty Samson. The "torch of foxes," an allusive image, unites arson, holidays, weddings, promiscuity, and decay with Biblical religion. What is to be made of this union depends on what can be made of the poem as a whole. In any case this image, freighted with meanings, functions complexly throughout the poem.

One final allusive image, an example of Thomas' craft at its most devious, deserves attention. "Especially when the October wind" (pp. 19-20) concerns the creation of poetry. The narrator, walking "By the sea's side," hears the natural noises and sees the familiar sights of his world, and finds in them a new sort of poetry.

> Some let me make you of the vowelled beeches,
> Some of the oaken voices, from the roots
> Of many a thorny shire tell you notes,
> Some let me make you of the water's speeches.

The poetry he desires is a process of recovering the essential qualities of the outside world and bringing them into the "tower of words" in which the poet, trapped by language and only faintly apprehending reality, resides. An allusive image is used to express this idea:

> Shut, too, in a tower of words, I mark
> On the horizon walking like the trees
> The wordy shapes of women . . . .

These lines recall Jesus' healing of the blind man at Bethsaida, who, asked whether he saw anything after a first treatment, replied, "I see men as trees, walking."

85

Thomas, looking at women, sees them "walking like the trees." This conceit, suggesting itself by the waving motion of distant trees, is not unusual. However, a supporting pun and an earlier draft version confirm the Biblical basis of this allusion. "I mark," puns Thomas; for the encounter at Bethsaida is recorded only in Mark (8:22-26). The earlier draft version of these lines reads:

> Shut in a tower of words, I mark
> Men in the distance walk like trees
> And talking as the four winds talk.[11]

A more exact Biblical reference, the draft uses "men" instead of "women," and includes, several lines later, "a blind man."

Maybe more than the other allusive images cited above, this last example demonstrates an essential proposition concerning the second type of imagery, which is that an allusive image does not necessarily make any religious statement within the realm of its poem. In fact, "Especially when the October wind" has already been mentioned as an example of a secular poem. This simile of women like trees operates in its own dimension to create a larger simile for the narrator's experience. Looking at humanity, he sees it as nature; so, laying aside the "syllabic blood" of ordinary poetry and draining away the words of ordinary human discourse, he tries a new poetry that can speak this new language. This poem expresses in poetry the attitude Thomas often expressed in prose: poetry should not be an application of words to a thing, but a creation of the thing wrought out of words. "Shut . . . in a tower of

[11] *The Notebooks of Dylan Thomas*, ed. Ralph Maud (New York, 1966), p. 348.

words," he would be like "the realistic novelist—Bennett, for instance" that he described to Miss Johnson; but, free from a mere "syllabic blood," and open to the language of the "vowelled beeches" and the "dark-vowelled birds," he could instead, "like Shelley," be "his medium first."[12]

Taking Biblical allusion into account yields a further dimension: like a blind man recovering from a disease and regaining a world of vision that should have been his all along, the narrator here frees himself from the bonds of language—he was, according to the draft, "chained by syllables hand and foot"—and encounters a less adulterated reality. But this dimension adds no Biblically religious significance. Although magic ("chemic blood") may be present, no notion of a Christian miracle inheres in this poem. Secularized, Saint Mark's report becomes a parable for Thomas' experience, providing paradigm without implying faith.

Why, it may be asked, did Thomas choose to speak in such devious ways? If a relationship between poetry and Bible can be inferred, why was it not simply stated? Such questions, asked of any who speak in parable, were asked of Jesus, who replied: "Therefore speak I to them in parables: because they seeing see not; and hearing they hear not, neither do they understand" (Matthew 13:13). Simply understood, this reply divulges a great truth about poetry: simple, easily comprehended poetry is often glanced at once, passed over, and quickly forgotten, while the ambiguous and opaque is often studied carefully, exposited at length, and consequently imprinted in the memory. Understood in a slightly deeper sense, the reply also suggests that parable teaches more forcefully than dictum, and that an en-

12 See above, pp. 12-13.

gaging narrative may be worth a thousand disengaged morals. But the heart of Jesus' reply finds expression in another part of his answer to the question. Jesus agreed to explain his meaning only to the disciples, "Because," as he said, "it is given unto you to know the mysteries of the kingdom of heaven, but to them it is not given" (Matthew 13:11). These "mysteries of the kingdom of heaven," not simple matters, are the subject of perceptions that, in revelation, go beyond the powers of language: for, as Paul observes (I Corinthians 2:9-10), "Eye hath not seen, nor ear heard. . . . But God has revealed them unto us. . . ." These "mysteries," not amenable to a direct portraiture, can be sketched only by metaphor. For metaphor, expressing one thing in terms of another, can paint the unknown in colors that are known, and comes as close as anything to an expression of the mysterious. And parable, aimed at apprehending the mysterious, is extended metaphor.

Through the use of such metaphors, Thomas worked to express these relationships between known and unknown. The disguise involved in his allusive imagery is no superficial sneakiness intended simply to ambush the rapid reader and waylay him in obscurity, nor is it any underhanded removal of obvious marks of identification designed to pass off the ordinary as the rare. An allusive image is not merely an amputated reference. Instead, the disguise presumes that, in fact, "they [the readers] seeing see not," that a plain sight of an object would by no means result in a plain comprehension of that object, and that, finally, there are ways of seeing, hearing, and comprehending, other than those evinced in the material or materialistically poetic worlds, to which the usual gradations "plain" or "obscure" do not apply. Good poetry, as Thomas reminded Miss Johnson, is not necessarily simple poetry.

The disguise, then, is intrinsic to the allusive image, expressing by its conjunction of many things what the many things, separate, could never quite say. While the "mysteries of the kingdom of heaven" are not usually the specific subject matter of allusive images, they are present insofar as an allusive image connects the Bible with the rest of the poem's reality. For the Bible, the narratives of which form a kind of giant parable concerning "the kingdom of heaven," has as its goal the illumination of these mysteries. A reference to the Bible suggests an interest in this parable, an interest that, even when not specifically religious, implies that this parable has a place in the questions asked by the poet.

The very fact that twentieth-century questions can be phrased in Biblical terms hints at the timeless nature of the questions. This timelessness suggests, for Thomas, that the narratives themselves are timeless and contemporary. Allusive imagery, we have seen, leads Thomas to notions of coexistence: Adam, for example, seems a very present figure. This coexistence, however, follows no theological creed. It is based neither on a notion of hypostatic union nor on a belief in Adam as Christ's mortal opposite present in all sinning mankind. In other words, it is not a dogmatic extension of Paul's statement that "as in Adam all die, even so in Christ shall all be made alive" (I Corinthians 15:22). For all its Biblical reference, this notion of coexistence is the result of poetic, rather than religious, logic, a logic concerned with archetypal significance that is more metaphorical than metaphysical. Any archetype, Biblical or otherwise, can function in this way: it can be argued, for example, that Helen, archetypal metaphor for the Maud Gonne figure of Yeats's "No Second Troy," establishes the contemporaneity of Ireland and Ilium. But neither this poem nor the Thomas poems discussed above demand of the poet a religious conviction about or a faith in the archetype.

That Bible affects image, there can be no doubt. And that image affects Bible, bringing the poet's particular interpretation to Biblical incident, should be equally clear. But what the place of Biblical religion may be in Thomas' poetry cannot be answered by a study of allusive imagery alone. The number of images found, and the insistence with which they are presented, may lead to speculation. But any conclusions must consider not only the evidence of referential and allusive images— which, after all, many poets may use many times for many reasons—but especially the evidence of thematic imagery.

Thematic Imagery

Thematic imagery is propositional; its theme can be expressed in sentence form as a proposition. This statement is not meant to suggest that Thomas began with a proposition such as "God is everywhere" and from that deduced his imagery. It means that there are discoverable propositions behind his thematic imagery, propositions not propounded at the outset of Thomas' poetic career but manifested in the process of writing. For a poet, like Cassirer's scientist, historian, and philosopher, "lives with his objects only as language presents them to him."[1] Before he can discover objects, especially such objects as propositions, he must have evolved a language to present them. In Thomas' work, this evolution can be charted by examining his thematic imagery.

The difficulty in a propositional approach to poetry is to discover the most useful propositions. "Useful" is a word very different from "correct." Numerous propositions may be found that do no violence to logic, so long as the logic is restricted within certain limits. They are correct propositions—as far as they go. But usefulness challenges the reader to discover the most universal, general propositions that correctly describe a large number of examples. This criterion of usefulness suggests that propositions are normally in a critic's, not a poet's, province. Whether or not Thomas was aware that certain of his images cohered into larger statements

[1] Ernst Cassirer, *Language and Myth*, trans. Susanne K. Langer (New York, 1946), p. 28.

is not of central importance. As long as the propositions that a critic discovers are useful—as long as they help replace obscurity with comprehension—it hardly matters whether Thomas wrote out of a position of exact propositional definition or out of a vague (or what is called "subconscious") awareness of larger patterns.

The line "Nor blaspheme down the stations of the breath" (from "A Refusal to Mourn," p. 112) constitutes a thematic image: making no Biblical reference or allusion, it unites an image from church tradition (the stations of the cross) with the pervasive theme that poetry (breath) is, in certain situations, irreverent. From it, certain propositions may be inferred. The simplest will be those stated in the language of the image; others will be more generalized. Here are some possible propositions:

(1) To pervert sacred language is to blaspheme. ("Stations of the cross" is here perverted to "stations of the breath.")

(2) To reduce a symbol of holiness to a symbol of mortality is to blaspheme. (This is a variation of number 1.)

(3) To live is to progress sequentially from one station to the next. (Breath equals life; life has stations like those of the cross.)

(4) Life is a torturous journey. (The stations of life are as difficult as Jesus' last journey.)

(5) Everyman's life is like Jesus'.

(6) Everyman is Christ.

(7) To curse is to destroy life. (Like "blow down" or "knock down," "blaspheme down" means "destroy.")

(8) Poetry is blasphemy.

(9) Life is blasphemy.

This list, readily expandable, contains propositions that correctly interpret this image. Many of them, however, ignoring context, contribute nothing to an understanding of either the poem as a whole or the body of Thomas' work. A poet could be imagined whose major theme, reappearing throughout his work, was that the language of church tradition must be kept pure. Were that poet to use this image, the first and second propositions given above would be very useful: they would cover a number of cases, of which this image would be one. Likewise, a poet inordinately concerned with cursing might best be comprehended by means of the seventh proposition, or perhaps the ninth. Is Thomas either of these poets? Examining this image alone, out of its context, cannot answer this question. Only by an extended study of a number of poems can the most useful propositions be singled out. A thematic image, drawing on themes that develop throughout a poet's work, provides the ideal subject for such a study.

"In country sleep" (pp. 181-186), one of Thomas' last poems, ends on just such a masterful image: "Your faith as deathless as the outcry of the ruled sun" (p. 186). Like the earlier example of thematic imagery—"The cureless counted body" from the poem "Holy Spring"— this line includes neither direct Biblical reference nor veiled Biblical allusion. Its religious significance results rather from association. Not directed at the Bible, it refers to other images and themes that are themselves of religious significance.

Central to this image is "sun," a word that, in the progression of Thomas' work, accumulates religious meanings. Delighting in polarities, Thomas was a poet of opposites: life and death, light and dark, youth and age, pair themselves in distinctive contrast throughout his work. These pairs are frequently paralleled, so that a common significance pervades life, light, youth, and opposes itself to the significance of death, dark, and age.

Life and death, ubiquitous topics, find expression in Thomas' imagery of wombs and tombs, birth and decease, and in such syntheses of these as "A process in the weather of the heart," a poem concerning the process, inherent in every living thing, that impels it inexorably towards death.

> A process in the eye forewarns
> The bones of blindness; and the womb
> Drives in a death as life leaks out.
>
> (p. 6)

Blindness signifies loss of light and hence of life; for light and dark, a familiar pair, are metaphors for life and death. In Thomas, as in Genesis, the coming of light to a darkened world signals the beginning of life. Light is also metaphor for the power of understanding; for words, the tools of understanding, illuminate the world. "In the beginning," quotes Thomas from John 1:1, "was the word,"

> . . . the word
> That from the solid bases of the light
> Abstracted all the letters of the void.
>
> (p. 27)

And "Do not go gentle into that good night," a villanelle, repeats in refrain the title line and the line "Rage, rage against the dying of the light" (p. 128); here, "that good night" (death) plainly opposes "light" (life).

Like life and death, light and dark are often united. Birth, result of "the short spark in a shapeless country"

(p. 80), produces offspring like the boys of "I see the boys of summer," whose fiery sparks unite all sorts of opposites. An image of this unity is the phrase "sons of flint and pitch" (p. 3): these boys, combining hard, light-colored, fire-making mineral with soft, black, flammable organic substance, live in life's conflagration. Not only "sons" of these opposites—born, in fact, of the copulation of antitheses expressed in "the poles are kissing as they cross" (p. 3)—these boys are also *suns of flint and pitch*," light-producing, life-giving balls of flame. This familiar pun of "sun" on "son," and of "son" on "sun," hallmarks a Thomas poem: he continually heard each of these in the other and, sensitive to the sound of words, bent himself to the creation of a poetry for the ear as well as the understanding.[2] The allusive image that serves as paradigm in this study—"My aris-

[2] " 'The Death of the Ear,' " wrote Thomas, "would be an apt subtitle for a book on the plight of modern poetry." Desiring "poetry that can be pronounced and read aloud," he decried contemporary poetry as "abominable," and complained of "this lack of aural value and this debasing of an art that is primarily dependent on the musical mingling of vowels and consonants. . . ." (Review of *The Solitary Way*, by William Soutar, *Squared Circle*, by William Montgomerie, and *Thirty Pieces*, by Sydney Salt, in *The Adelphi*, VIII [September 1934], 418-420.) Thomas' concern with "aural value"—the sort of value that fuses "sun" and "son," and creates an absolute ambiguity in which one word does the work of two—is evidenced by his interest and expertise in reading and recording his poetry. Which is not to say that Thomas has invented a novel pun. Puns on "son" and "sun" abound in English poetry, and probably antedate this anonymous thirteenth-century lyric:

> Nou goth sonne under wode
> Me reweth, Marie, thi faire rode
> Nou goth sonne under tre
> Me reweth, Marie, thi sone and the.

ing prodigal / Sun the father"—manifests this union of
son and sun, as do such lines as "Your polestar neigh-
bor, sun of another street" ("Deaths and Entrances,"
p. 129), and "The substance forked that marrowed the
first sun" ("In the beginning," p. 27), in which Adam
is "first *son*." Son, implicitly contrasted with father, sug-
gests youth. Throughout his work Thomas returned to
visions of his boyhood. Many of the stories in *Portrait
of the Artist as a Young Dog* reveal a consciousness of
youth in contrast with age: Uncle Jim in "The Peaches,"
Grandpa in "A Visit to Grandpa's," the Jenkyns and the
Bevans in "The Fight," and Mr. Farr in "Old Garbo,"
all standing as figures of parental authority, insist on
the youth of the protagonist; and an awareness of the
family he has temporarily fled never deserts the rebel-
lious young narrator of "Just Like Little Dogs" and
"Who Do You Wish Was With Us?" And such poems
as "Once it was the colour of saying," "Poem in Octo-
ber," "The Hunchback in the Park," and "Fern Hill"
recall the security of youth and suggest the depreda-
tions of age.

Light, life, and father-son relationships are all im-
plicit in another common equation in Thomas' poetry,
that of son and Son. Jesus Christ, Son of God, is a son
like the poet and a heavenly light-giver like the sun.
"Dawn Raid" ends with an allusive image that evinces
this equation: "a hundred storks perch on the sun's
right hand" (p. 152). At the ascension, Jesus Christ
"was received up into heaven, and sat on the right
hand of God" (Mark 16:19). Like Father, Son dispenses
right-handed judgment and mercy in the case of this
hundred-year-old man killed in a fire raid: the hundred
storks, image of the hundred birthdays (since stork is
an emblem of birth), apotheosize this elderly gentle-

man through the Son's intervention. "On the Marriage of a Virgin," a poem deserving some attention, forges this link between "sun" and Son. Mixing images of Danae with those of Jesus, this sonnet tells of a virgin waking after her wedding night while "this day's sun leapt up the sky out of her thighs" (p. 141). Allusive images confirm the presence of Son, who, after feeding the multitude with five loaves and two fishes, walked on the water of the Sea of Galilee (John 6): for virginity, in this poem, is "old as loaves and fishes" and miraculous as "the shipyards of Galilee's footprints." Sun is also husband: "For a man sleeps where fire leapt down and she learns through his arm / That other sun, the jealous coursing of the unrivalled blood" (p. 141). That Son is sun can be seen in many poems, among them "Vision and Prayer," in which

> . . . the loud sun
> Christens down
> The sky
>
> (p. 165)

and in which

> . . . the high noon
> Of his wounds
> Blinds my
> Cry.
>
> (p. 157)

Understanding's light is brightest at noon; and Jesus was the "high noon" of time, its brightest moment. The crucifixion, time of Jesus' wound, was the Son's most intense time: for this reason the "crucifixion on the mountain" in "Altarwise by owl-light" is described as

"Time's nerve in vinegar" and the "moutain minute" (p. 84).

Thomas, seeing himself as son, also saw himself as Son.

> I was a mortal to the last
> Long breath that carried to my father
> The message of his dying christ.

> You who bow down at cross and altar,
> Remember me and pity Him
> Who took my flesh and bone for armour
> And doublecrossed my mother's womb.
>                     ("Before I knocked," p. 9)

This referential image ("his dying christ") announces the identity in no uncertain terms. Less certain is the identity of son, sun, and Son established in the "sons of flint and pitch" examined earlier; sons (boys) and suns (fires), these are also Sons, by virtue of a preceding allusive image:

> In spring we cross our foreheads with the holly,
> Heigh ho the blood and berry,
> And nail the merry squires to the trees.
>                     (p. 3)

In imitation of Jesus, but confusing the florae of Christmas and Easter, the boys don a thorny crown of holly and become Sons. The "poles" that are "kissing as they cross" are, in this dimension, not antithetical polarities but the horizontal and vertical members of the cross, coming together to crucify them. It is in "Poem in October," however, that the blending of these three meanings is handled with consummate skill: Son, son, and sun are, here, equivalent alternatives.

And I saw in the turning so clearly a child's
Forgotten mornings when he walked with his mother
      Through the parables
        Of sun light.

                  (p. 114)

In the final thematic image from "In country sleep,"
then, the word "sun" can claim—by association with
other uses of the word in Thomas' poetry—a religious
significance. But a thematic image demands a contex-
tual interpretation. How does the poem itself justify
the identification of "sun" and "Son"?

"In country sleep," not unlike Yeats's "A Prayer for
My Daughter" in subject, is a meditation at the bedside
of a sleeping child. Fairy tales and ritualistic imagery
fuse to create a sacred aura. "The country is holy,"
claims Thomas famously: no rude pantheism, this holi-
ness derives from Christian images and a basic Chris-
tian theme within the poem.

A hill touches an angel! Out of a saint's cell
The nightbird lauds through nunneries and domes of leaves

Her robin breasted tree, three Marys in the rays.
*Sanctum sanctorum* the animal eye of the wood
In the rain telling its beads. . . .

                  (p. 182)

Two orders of images function in this passage: there are
those which allude to church tradition, and those which
allude to the Bible. Of the first order, "the rain telling
its beads" describes rainfall in terms of a traditional
sacramental image. The "saint's cell," "nunneries," and
"domes of leaves," more traditional than Biblical, all
describe architecture; and this architectural motif con-

nects them with the specifically Biblical "*sanctum sanctorum*" (Holy of Holies). The Holy of Holies, as described in the Bible (Exodus 26:33, Hebrews 9:3, and elsewhere), denotes the innermost sanctuary of a tabernacle or temple. A central location, this *sanctum sanctorum* is the "animal eye" in this woods: suggesting better-than-human sight, it also describes the center (like the *eye* of a storm) for the *anima*, or soul. Like "cell" and "dome," "*sanctum sanctorum*" suggests that "The country is holy" because a place of worship has been constructed. The "robin breasted tree, three Marys in the rays" seems a visual image connected with church tradition, perhaps a picture of a cross shedding the light of its glory on three mourning women. Red with the blood of Jesus' wound, the cross is "robin breasted"; the phrase also suggests the robbers crucified with Jesus, and, contextually, both an actual tree full of robins and Robin Hood, fabled thief whose name recalls the Little Red Riding Hood allusions in the poem. Although there are six Marys in the New Testament, these "three Marys" are probably Mary Magdalene and Mary the mother of James (both of whom witnessed the crucifixion and resurrection) and the Virgin.[3] The hill that "touches an angel," along with other elements of praise offered by nature, is identifiably Biblical. That nature praises God is a common theme in the Psalms, and is concentrated in Psalm 148:

[3] Mary of Bethany, sister of Lazarus, may be suggested here, especially if "rays" is taken as "raise." Mary Magdalene and Mary the mother of James witnessed the "raising" of Jesus, as Mary of Bethany the "raising" of Lazarus. The point, founded on pun and built out of quibble, is unimportant as long as the fact of Biblical reference in "three Marys" is clear.

Praise ye him, all his angels: praise ye him, all his hosts.
Praise ye him, sun and moon: praise ye him, all ye
    stars of light. . . .

. . . . . . . . . . . . . . . . . .   . . . . . . . . . . . . . . . .

Praise the Lord from the earth, ye dragons, and all
    deeps:
Fire, and hail; snow, and vapour; stormy wind fulfilling
    his word:
Mountains, and all hills; fruitful trees, and all cedars:
Beasts, and all cattle; creeping things, and flying fowl.

Not only from animals does Thomas' praise come. The
elements themselves rejoice: "Earth, air, water, fire,
singing into the white act" (p. 185), recall the Psalms.
References, then, establish a Biblical tone. But "sun,"
to be of thematic importance, should refer specifically
to Jesus. Is Jesus a part of this poem?

"In country sleep" tells of a Thief who comes stealing
in during the night. Comforting the daughter with as-
surances of what this Thief will not do, the poem also
warns against what he will certainly do. "Ever and
ever he finds a way," Part I ends, "as the snow falls,"

> . . . as the winged
> Apple seed glides,
> And falls, and flowers in the yawning wound at our sides,
> As the world falls, silent as the cyclone of silence.
>                         (p. 183)

Apple, fall, and wound bring Adam to mind, whose
"wound"—the removal of his rib and the creation of
Eve—led through the apple to his fall. As all men, for
Thomas, are of Adam, so in every man's wound flowers
the apple seed that, grown to tree's size and found by

*101*

woman, leads to the world's fall. But the "yawning wound at our sides," intimating Thomas' favorite I-am-Christ identity, suggests both Jesus' wound during the crucifixion and the redemption from the apple-flowering sin of Adam. An earlier allusion adumbrates Jesus: "and the soul walks / The waters shorn" (p. 183). Jesus, famous walker of the waters, adopted the identity of shepherd and warned of the thief: "He that entereth not by the door into the sheepfold, but climbeth up some other way, the same is a thief and a robber. . . . I am the door of the sheep. All that ever came before me are thieves and robbers: but the sheep did not hear them. I am the door: by me if any man enter in, he shall be saved, and shall go in and out, and find pasture. The thief cometh not, but for to steal, and to kill, and to destroy . . ." (John 10:1, 7-10). He further warned of the wolf: "he that is an hireling, and not the shepherd, whose own the sheep are not, seeth the wolf coming, and leaveth the sheep, and fleeth: and the wolf catcheth them, and scattereth the sheep" (John 10:12). Thomas, spinning his own parable from similar threads, discounts the danger of the "wolf in a sheepwhite hood" and (with a glance at the windy wolf in the fable of the three little pigs) "the roarer at the latch." "Fear most," he says,

> For ever of all not the wolf in his baaing hood
> Nor the tusked prince, in the ruttish farm, at the rind
> And mire of love, but the Thief as meek as the dew.
>
> (p. 182)

This Thief, inconclusive symbol for all the unspecified dangers that beset the growing up of a little girl, may be death, husband, God, or simply growth itself and consequent loss of youth. He comes to steal "not her tide raking / Wound, nor her riding high, nor her eyes, nor kindled hair" (p. 186); no mere carnal intruder, this Thief ignores her physical attractions.[4] He comes instead to steal

> . . . her faith that each vast night and the saga of prayer
>                                                 He comes to take
> Her faith that this last night for his unsacred sake
> He comes to leave her in the lawless sun awaking
>
> Naked and forsaken to grieve he will not come.
>                                                 (p. 186)

This maze of logic, best untangled from the bottom upwards, means the following:

(A) She believes (lines 3-5 above) that tonight at last he comes to awaken her to the realization of grief.

(B) However (lines 1 and 2 above), she has faith that each night he comes to destroy this belief. (Negation of A: therefore she will not be awakened to grief.)

(C) But actually he comes to steal the faith expressed in lines 1 and 2. (Negation of B and consequent affirmation of A.)

The Thief, then, "comes to leave her in the lawless sun awaking / Naked and forsaken to grieve he will not come." Like a forgotten dream, the stimulus that wakes

---

[4] Whether from misprint or misreading, Thomas recorded "riding *thigh*" in place of "riding high" in his reading of "In country sleep" on *Dylan Thomas Reading*, vol. i (Caedmon TC 1043). This mistake perhaps indicates the type of associations Thomas made between assonant words; in any case "riding thigh," whether originally written as the actual phrase or intended merely as a kind of pun behind "riding high," fits neatly into the sexual imagery of this line.

*103*

the girl vanishes from her memory: although wakened
by the Thief's coming, she is unaware of the cause, and
grieves to think that he has not come. This Thief, no
good man ("unsacred sake," "lawless sun," and "naked
and forsaken" all describe his effects), seems arch-
hypocrite. He steals the one protection most essential:
her sense of danger. So insidious are his designs that
she, grieving over his absence, remains convinced that
his coming is desirable. Which is why the poem, a
warning, must be written.

Jesus warned of the apparent similarity between thief
and shepherd. Thomas, pointing out the possibility of
this fatal confusion, distinguishes between them in the
final thematic image. Thief, earlier, brought "lawless
sun"; but the poem ends with "ruled sun." If son is
Son, "ruled" means "according to rule," or heeding the
mandates of God. It can mean "overruled" or "con-
trolled": in this sense, sun and Son are subjected to
patterns, the one of rising and setting, the other death
and resurrection. If "ruled" suggests the wooden stick
of a measuring rule, it also suggests the wooden stick
of the cross: sun marks off the day as a ruler marks off a
page, and Son, on the ruler of the cross, takes the meas-
ure of man and delineates the Christian's course. In any
case, this "ruled sun" is the antithesis of the "lawless
sun" of the Thief.

The allusion to crucifixion is confirmed by the re-
maining words of this final line. The "outcry of the
ruled sun" is the voice of the dying Jesus; "naked and
forsaken" on the cross for the "unsacred sake" of in-
different humanity, he cried (according to Mark 15:34)
"Eloi, Eloi, lama sabachthani?" Thomas, familiar with
the cry, had heard it before:

I hear, through dead men's drums, the riddled lads,
Strewing their bowels from a hill of bones,
Cry Eloi to the guns.

("My world is pyramid," p. 36)

This outcry is "deathless." For Thomas, a poet of proc-
ess, very few things are deathless. Those which achieve
immortality do so through a religious apotheosis. "And
death shall have no dominion," writes the young
Thomas, echoing the Pauline explanation of the eternal
life.[5] Those which die engage in a perpetual motion
associated with sun and Son: "Break in the sun till the
sun breaks down, / And death shall have no dominion"
(p. 77). Refusing to mourn the death of a child, Thomas
echoes both this Biblical passage and another ("he that
overcometh shall not be hurt of the second death,"
Revelation 2:11) in the line "After the first death, there
is no other" (p. 112). The ambiguity in this line—does
it express faith in eternal life after death, or does it
deny that there is anything more after death?—resolves
into a single affirmation when read contextually and
thematically. The affirmation, however, does not deny
death. That final result of life's process remains; but
faith or memory of eternity overcomes it. Through a
similar apotheosis, the women and their lovers of "In
the white giant's thigh" become the "Hale dead and
deathless" (p. 199): buried in the body, they yet live in
the spirit of Thomas' poem.

In the final image from "In country sleep," it is "faith"
that is "deathless." This conjunction of words leads, by

[5] "For he that is dead is freed from sin. Now if we be dead
with Christ, we believe that we shall also live with him: knowing
that Christ being raised from the dead dieth no more; death
hath no more dominion over him" (Romans 6:7-9).

a kind of dislocation Thomas enjoyed using, to "Your *death* as *faithless* as the outcry of the ruled sun."[6] Jesus' cry on the cross does, indeed, seem faithless: yet, for a Christian, the words express less apostasy than despair, less dereliction than sorrow. A superb integration of matter and medium, the words here catch the topics of appearance and hypocrisy that inform the poem, and suggest that Jesus' death only *appears* faithless. In fact, it was not; and, in fact, the words are not "death" and "faithless" but "faith" and "deathless." The "faith" here, no Christian belief, is the daughter's misled faith in the Thief. She will awake "from country sleep, this dawn and each first dawn," with her faith intact. Making no attempt to disabuse her of her convictions—to do so would be as futile as attempting to shake her faith in the "hearthstone tales" of children's fables—the poet instead offers parable. "The country is holy"; but the Thief is not. Why these two elements, of natural prayer on the one hand and Thief and daughter on the other, are present in this poem provides a challenge to the reader. This sort of obscurity of relationship demands attention; its resolution, not immediately apparent, is contained in the religious image of the last line.

Like Jesus' cry from the cross (Thomas' simile reads), so the faith of his daughter. Deathless, it lives in an eternity separate from the mere corporeality of life. The daughter's faith, like Jesus' "lama sabachthani" ("Why hast thou forsaken me"), supposes that she, too, is forsaken. Yet it is Jesus' outcry that exposes the specious

[6] Thomas enjoyed this kind of inversion, using it to good effect in such phrases as "Altarwise by owl-light" (which suggests "owl-wise by altarlight"), "tide-tongued" (which suggests "tongue-tied"), and "the man in the wind and the west moon" (which suggests "the man in the moon and the west wind).

world of the temple to the power of Christianity. "Jesus cried with a loud voice," reports Mark (15:37-38), "And the veil of the temple was rent in twain. . . ." The "veil of the temple" refers to the curtain that, in Hebrew tabernacles and temples, separated the holy place from the Most Holy Place, the Holy of Holies or *sanctum sanctorum*. The *sanctum sanctorum* was intended to house the Ark of the Covenant, a chest believed to contain the tablets of the Law. Opening this "animal eye of the wood" (in the temple constructed in the first part of the poem) to view, this "outcry of the ruled sun" fuses the two disparate elements of this poem—the descriptions of holy countryside and those of daughter and Thief—into one moving statement of faith. "In this tearing of the veil of the temple which separated the holy place from the Holy of Holies," writes Halford E. Luccock, ". . . men have found a picturesque symbol of a profound truth of Christian experience and history. It is the truth so powerfully expressed in Hebrews, that the crucifixion of Jesus, his sacrificial death, removed all that separated man from God, 'the new and living way which he opened for us through the curtain' (Heb. 10:20)."[7]

Yeats, ending his prayer for his daughter, asked "How but in custom and in ceremony / Are innocence and beauty born?"[8] Thomas ends this meditation on the innocence and beauty of his "girl riding far and near" with the custom and ceremony of Christianity, which, interceding against the Thief, assures her that "you shall awake from country sleep, this dawn and each first dawn, / Your faith as deathless as the outcry of the ruled sun." This intercession is her protection from wolf

---

[7] *The Interpreter's Bible*, vii (1951), 907.
[8] *Poems*, p. 187.

and Thief. For, according to the promise of the Son, "I am the door: by me if any man enter in, he shall be saved, and shall go in and out, and find pasture"; the wolf, and whatever danger this allegorical beast suggests, will no longer threaten.

From the point of view of literary criticism there are differences in technique that distinguish our analyses of these three types of religious imagery. Referential imagery, clearly, can be analyzed with very little concern for context. A reader, observing the image itself and relating it to its Biblical source, is well on his way to a thorough understanding of its function; several summary statements about the work as a whole can then clarify the relationship of image and work. The explication of an allusive image involves the reader in a broader analysis. Image and Bible are still the primary coordinates; but more detailed knowledge of Thomas' work, introduced because of the depth of disguise possible in this second type of imagery, is required to define the exact function.

Finally, as this chapter's discussion of thematic imagery confirms, any thorough analysis of this third type engages the reader in an examination not only of the work itself but of the topics, themes, and images of a number of other works. So comprehensive are the implications of such an image, in fact, that, while a complete examination of each thematic image is entirely unmanageable, an exhaustive examination of one is bound to uncover the central thematic considerations underlying the others.

The increasing dependence on context that is observable within these three types of imagery suggests that there is also an increasing capacity for involved and pertinent statement about religion. Contradicting *prima facie* evidence that obvious religious imagery signals profound religious statement, the method developed here for studying Thomas' poetry rather suggests the reverse: that Thomas, when referring less, said more. Confirming this hypothesis, the examination of individual poems in the subsequent chapters of this study develops one remarkable conclusion: Thomas, in the course of time, became a poet increasingly involved with religion, and increasingly willing to express, in his poetry, this deep involvement.

🎵 *PART THREE*     The Parables of
Sun Light

Dylan Thomas' *Collected Poems* comprises, with minor variations, his five published volumes of poetry: *18 Poems* (1934), *Twenty-five Poems* (1936), *The Map of Love* (1939), *Deaths and Entrances* (1946), and *In Country Sleep* (1952). The poems gathered into each of these volumes reflect an order that is something less than strictly chronological. A master of revision, Thomas put together a number of his published poems from earlier drafts that he had composed before he was twenty. Of the eighty-nine complete collected poems, forty-four are based on early work.[1]

The label "early poem," however, is not to be confused with "poem based on early work." Thomas revised extensively. Revision often reformed the entire expression of a poem. Any notions of chronology must therefore be founded not simply on the sequence of the original drafts but also on the sequence of revisions. While compiling his published volumes, Thomas subjected every entry to a critical scrutiny. Some passed nearly unchanged; some were altered almost beyond recognition. All, however, reflect his particular attitude at the time of revision. By reason of this attitude, the contents of *Collected Poems* can be taken as roughly chronological: if a consistent attitude or tone found in

[1] For a discussion of chronology in the genesis and revision of Thomas' poetry, see Ralph N. Maud, "Dylan Thomas' Collected Poems: Chronology of Composition," *PMLA*, LXXVI (June 1961), 292-297.

*18 Poems* is markedly different from an attitude or tone
that characterizes *Twenty-five Poems, 18 Poems* should
be considered an early work and *Twenty-five Poems* a
later work, and some development from one to the
other should be posited. For discretion, especially in
Thomas' case, is the better part of poetry; it was his
critical discretion that eventually reduced the earlier
outpourings of his fertile imagination to the order and
form of art. What Thomas blurted out in an uninhibited
relish of creation may be of interest to psychologists
and biographers; but what he shaped in the careful
craft of revision remains the object of the critic's at-
tention. The terms "early" and "late" then, must be
taken to refer to the chronology, not of drafts, but of
the final revisions that he approved for publication.

*18 Poems* is not remarkable as the work of a religious
poet. The concomitant requirements of religion—belief,
action, and obligation—are not met in this volume.
None of the poems suggests that formulated religious
thought prefaces its composition or is to be inferred
from its statements, none calls attention to the activity
of praise as a religious gesture, and none professes a
sense of commitment. Yet there is, in this volume, a dis-
tinctly Biblical ambience. Titles betray its presence:
"Where once the waters of your face," "In the begin-
ning," "Light breaks where no sun shines," and "I
dreamed my genesis" all carry Biblical allusion. Numer-
ous words in the poems further define this feature: the
word "Christ" appears three times in these eighteen
poems, as does "Adam"; "Jordan" appears twice; crosses,
sabbaths, altars, heavens, angels, and manna all are in
evidence; and two phrases ("quick and dead" and
"gives up its dead") refer directly to Acts 10:42 ("he
which was ordained of God to be the Judge of quick

and dead") and Revelation 20:13 ("And the sea gave up the dead which were in it").

Upon examination, this ambience reveals itself to be the result of referential and allusive imagery. In *18 Poems*, Thomas' concern was less with religion as theme than with Biblical imagery as metaphor. The boundary between these two is often indefinite, and the reader is often hard pressed to say just where Biblical religion stops being metaphor for the poet's experience and becomes, instead, the topic for which the poet's experience is a metaphor. Religion, not yet mistress of Thomas' poetry in this earliest volume, is still a handmaiden.

Religious imagery in *18 Poems* provides metaphors for Thomas' central subject: himself. Professor Tindall observes that these poems, "generally of what he agreed to call his 'womb-tomb period,'" are concerned with "creation, both physical and poetic, and the temporal process of birth, death, and rebirth. . . ."[2] The great narratives of the Bible—especially those of the Creation and of the life of Jesus—similarly concern these subjects. Confirming both the universality and the significance of his own experiences, the poet (who appears as first person in thirteen of these poems and implicitly in at least two others) identifies himself with Biblical archetypes. Having been created, the poet creates; Adam, subject of the original Creation, also creates; so poet resembles Adam, and the story of the poet's creation rephrases Genesis. The poet, suffering, is martyred and reborn; Jesus, suffering, was crucified and resurrected; so the poet resembles Jesus, and paints his own existence in the Gospels' colors. Narrative, rather than faith, is involved here; for young Thomas, less

[2] *Reader's Guide*, p. 27.

explicit about holy praise than secular process, drew from the Gospels not the divinity of the Christ but the humanity of Jesus as his parallel.

This emphasis on the Bible as narrative rather than as religious authority manifests itself in Thomas' early imagery. Thematic imagery is absent here, because such images demand a kind of total religious context absent from these poems. Referential and allusive images abound. The identity of poet and Jesus, a common topic in this volume, appears in poems that otherwise involve religious matters only tangentially. Yet this identity is part of a way of speaking, a language that Thomas is anxious to establish. In "When once the twilight locks no longer"—a poem that is, in Olson's words, "a meditation on the origin of the idea of death"[3] —the poet describes his "creature" (himself) as one who is familiar with death's language: "He had by heart the Christ-cross-row of death" (p. 4). "Christ-cross-row," as dictionaries tell, means alphabet. "Alphabet," in fact, could replace "Christ-cross-row" in both meaning and meter. Why the circumlocution? The poem ends with the phrase "worlds hang on the trees." Taking the tree as the cross suggests that Christ is the world. Jesus, dying, saved others, and overcame the futility of a life that might otherwise seem to lead only to death. The language of death learned here by the poet is related to the death of Jesus: in other words, it is not entirely destructive or hopeless. This poem, neither praise nor prayer, makes no religious statement beyond this one. It presumes upon a common convention: Jesus died that others might live. This proposition, for many, is a tenet of faith. In this poem, all that can be said is that it provides a metaphor for the topics of

[3] *The Poetry of Dylan Thomas*, p. 36.

the poem, which, whatever else they may be, are not particularly religious.

"If I were tickled by the rub of love," another poem of birth and death, is also about language. "Man be my metaphor," explains Thomas, and one of the men he chooses is Jesus, "My Jack of Christ born thorny on the tree" (p. 15). "*My* Jack" implies identity of poet and Jesus, as does "Jack of Christ," which alludes to a similar identity in a Hopkins poem:

> I am all at once what Christ is, since he was what I am,
>      and
> This Jack . . .
>               Is immortal diamond.[4]

Christmas ("born") and Good Friday ("thorny on the tree") fuse here as Biblical language again provides a way of seeing death in birth's terms and of reconciling the two.

Similar references and allusions are spotted throughout other poems in this volume. In "My world is pyramid," the "riddled lads" on "a hill of bones" cry "Eloi": these lads, dying, resemble Jesus. In "My hero bares his nerves," the bared nerve, connected to "wrist," serves both masturbation and the writing of adolescent poetry.

> He holds the wire from this box of nerves
> Praising the mortal error
> Of birth and death, the two sad knaves of thieves,
> And the hunger's emperor;
> He pulls the chain, the cistern moves.
>
>                     (p. 11)

---

[4] "That Nature is a Heraclitean Fire and of the comfort of the Resurrection," *Poems*, p. 105.

This allusive image of "thieves" and "emperor," suggesting the thieves flanking Jesus on Golgotha, also suggests the male genitals; once again the topic of birth and death is presented in a metaphor of the crucifixion.

Many of the other religious images in this volume have previously been noted as examples of referential or allusive imagery. The connection between "the face of the waters" and "Where once the waters of your face" has been examined, as has the connection between Genesis and "Light breaks where no sun shines"; the "apple" and "flood" of "If I were tickled by the rub of love" have been identified as Biblical allusions; the allusion to Saint Mark in "Especially when the October wind" has been studied, as has the "macadam" image of "When, like a running grave"; and the isolated allusive imagery of Adam and Samson has been explicated in the three final poems, "I dreamed my genesis," "My world is pyramid," and "All all and all the dry worlds lever."[5] Most of these eighteen poems make only incidental use of religious imagery. It plays, in this first volume, a supporting rather than a central role. Three poems, however, deserve closer attention: "I see the boys of summer," "Before I knocked," and "In the beginning."

"In the beginning" (pp. 27-28) is extended metaphor. The conceit reads simply: the creation of the world resembles the conception of the embryo. At all points, the equation works. Five stanzas, each introduced with the first three words of the Bible, present five coordinate explanations of the reduction of primeval chaos into ordered creation. The first, offering a sexual interpretation, depicts creation as the coming of the male "three

[5] For a discussion of "I fellowed sleep" see Appendix, pp. 216-217.

118

pointed star" to the "empty face." Creation is the coming of "one bough of bone" to "the rooting air"; it is also the coming of a "substance" that, in the verbs of Thomas' sexual idiom, both "forked" and "marrowed." The second stanza, partly sexual (if "crosstree" is male to the female "grail"), concerns language: the "signature," or creative Word, left "imprints on the water" and stamped a "minted face upon the moon." God, bringing dry land from the water, also created the moon. The sexual process, creating an embryo in the watery womb, impregnates the virgin: for moon is traditionally associated with virgin. The moon is also, as Professor Tindall notes, the Virgin Mary; and if the "imprints on the water" suggest Jesus on the Sea of Galilee (as in "the shipyards of Galilee's footprints," p. 141), the "minted face" stamped on the "moon" is a metaphor for Mary's conception. Once again, Jesus' history provides a paradigm for the poet's experience.

Stanza three, offering little Biblical material, seems rather to condense civilization's history into a progress from horse to automobile. The "mounting fire," in the beginning, "set alight" the "weathers"; does this fire, mounted, alight on equine withers? If these words suggest horse, the horseless carriage seems present in the "Life" that "*pumped* from the earth and rock / The secret *oils* that *drive* the grass" (italics added). Stanza four returns to the verbal creation of stanza two.

> In the beginning was the word, the word
> That from the solid bases of the light
> Abstracted all the letters of the void;

this unmistakable reference to the Gospel of John describes the Creation as an enlightenment brought about by language. The second half of this stanza's conceit, proving that the religious statement is more a metaphor than a subject, connects the Creation to the embryo's genesis.

> And from the cloudy bases of the breath
> The word flowed up, translating to the heart
> First characters of birth and death.

Like the earlier "Christ-cross-row of death," this language helps the born creature reconcile the fact of birth with the threat of death.

The final stanza, assembling man ("brain," "celled," "veins," "Blood"), ends with the "ribbed original of love." This allusive imagery connects the embryo, as product or "original" of love, with Adam. But the connection seems one of narrative and archetype rather than one of philosophy and ontology. This entire poem, imbued with Biblical language, posits a relationship between man's history and Bible stories; but any relationship between man's faith and Biblical religion is left to inference.

In "Before I knocked" (pp. 8-9), a prenatal voice discusses what Derek Stanford calls "the life of the child prior even to its conception."[6] Addressing the reader, this "I"—perhaps newborn babe, perhaps sperm cell—recounts existence in mythic terms.

> I who was shapeless as the water
> That shaped the Jordan near my home
> Was brother to Mnetha's daughter
> And sister to the fathering worm.

Less significant as character than as reference, Mnetha, a figure in *Tiriel*, suggests Blake's mythopoeic mind.

---

[6] *Dylan Thomas* (New York, 1954), p. 47.

*120*

Blake, rejecting accepted paradigms, coined new counters for the experience that he wished to express archetypally. Thomas' "I" begins his experience in an undifferentiated and androgynous state, making no more distinction between myth, Biblical or Blakean, than between sex, male or female. The burden of this poem is the resemblance of "I" and "christ":

> I was a mortal to the last
> Long breath that carried to my father
> The message of his dying christ.

While insisting on identity, the poem also preserves a distinction: "remember me and pity Him," the poet implores. The incarnation of the Christ in this world is, nevertheless, a personal experience: he took *"my* flesh and bone for armour," it was *"my* veins" that "flowed with the Eastern weather," and, like Jesus born of earthly Mary and Holy Ghost, "*I,* born of flesh and ghost, was neither / A ghost nor man, but mortal ghost" (italics added). Birth, likened to the crossing of an enemy frontier, is tantamount to crucifixion:

> And flesh was snipped to cross the lines
> Of gallow crosses on the liver
> And brambles in the wringing brains.

Several jokes, however, place the emphasis of this poem more on sex and the body than on religion and divinity. The "Jordan near my home"—the famous Biblical river near Jesus' home—may also be the infamous chamber pot that, when used by mother, is near the embryo's home. The final phrase, "doublecrossed my mother's womb," carries in its multitudinous meanings references to the crucifixion and betrayal as well as jokes about crossing the womb's entrance twice (once in, once out) and cheating Mary out of pleasure by an incorporeal conception.[7] Once again, Thomas seems less concerned with the divinity of the Christ than the humanity of Jesus, which he engages as a parallel for his own humanity. Images, referential and allusive only, cohere into no greater religious statement than the simple notion that Jesus' life resembles every man's; and even this identity is treated as something of a joke.

The relationship of religion to humor in Thomas' poetry would bear a thorough investigation. Perhaps because of the human desire to reduce the mysterious to the familiar, or to rise above the embarrassing power of the intimate by laughing at it, sex is a common subject of humor. Convention dictates that almost any sexual reference can be funny; but whether this humor involves the sniggering of the small-minded or the delight of the perceptive depends largely on the ability of the user of the sexual reference to place it functionally in his context. Much of the humor in Thomas' poetry is sexual, and most of it is well placed. And, as this study should make plain, many of Thomas' religious images have sexual overtones. When the sexual dimension is patently humorous, it tends to undercut the religious significance: although humor may sometimes be the wit that Eliot called "structural decoration of a serious idea" and "alliance of levity and seriousness," for Thomas it works less as a support to the religious dimension than as a digression from it.[8] His finest religious poems—those appearing later in his work—are poems of great beauty and high seriousness that contain little of this humor. They are still branded by the

[7] These interpretations are elaborated in Stanford, pp. 48-49.
[8] T. S. Eliot, "Andrew Marvell," *Selected Essays*, p. 296.

*122*

familiar blend of sex and religion, but the sex is no longer the subject for jokes.

Sex and religion help compose one of Thomas' most masterly poems: "I see the boys of summer" (pp. 1-3). Poles and crosses, as well as "tithings," "floods," "apples," and "Divide the night and day," confirm the presence of Biblical reference and allusion, as do the lines that establish the speakers as types of Christ:

> In spring we cross our foreheads with the holly,
> Heigh ho the blood and berry,
> And nail the merry squires to the trees.

The topics here seem to be birth, growth, prodigality, and death, presented in a debate between what William Moynihan aptly labels "the voice of restraint" and "the voice of revolt."[9] Metaphors are provided by the stories of the Creation and the crucifixion; but the poem, not fundamentally Biblical in its language, presents a number of coordinate analogies. One of these involves seasonal rhythms: "summer," "winter," and "night and day," as well as "harvest," "soils," "tides," "seedy," and "planted," suggest a pagan aspect. Metaphors of depth and darkness abound. Sun, moon, stars, and "world's ball" provide cosmic metaphors. While containing religious imagery, this poem diffuses its language through all these metaphors, and remains something other than an essentially religious statement.

A phrase from this poem, "sons of flint and pitch," has been examined as an element contributing to the "ruled sun" image of "In country sleep." Yet it seems inaccurate to label the phrase "sons of flint and pitch" a thematic image. For the presence of thematic imagery

[9] *The Craft and Art of Dylan Thomas*, p. 184.

presupposes major themes. In Thomas' case, as in the case of most poets, these themes did not spring up full-blown in his first poems. Evolution—the process through which a critical mind develops a poetic language by rejecting worthless ideas while seizing and elaborating the more valuable ones—requires time, time first to spin out a number of ideas, and time next to cull the sterile and save the productive. His earliest letters evince his desire to grapple with nothing less than the grandest and most significant topics of human experience: birth, death, love, God, and, above all, the enigma of himself. But the process of defining this desire in a manageable poetic language was no quick procedure.

The development of a poetic language included the development of Thomas' religious themes. Working towards a compact style, he made, of certain words, shorthand notations that express whole networks of ideas; "I like," he wrote to Charles Fisher, ". . . saying two things at once in one word, four in two and one in six. . . ."[10] But unless the reader is familiar with Thomas' later work (and such familiarity, after all, places the reader above chronology), the force of a word such as "sons" in the poem "I see the boys of summer" is apt to be missed. Which is not to say that Thomas, even in his earliest writings, did not perceive the vast possibilities of such a word. It is simply to say that he could not expect the word, limited to the context of only a few poems, to function with the full effect of his later thematic images. While presenting a number of Biblical images, the poems of *18 Poems* lack the kind of statement made possible by thematic imagery; for this reason, they can hardly justify being labeled "religious" poems.

[10] "February 1935," *Letters*, p. 151.

Mixed and subordinate though it may be, religious imagery is an omnipresent feature of *18 Poems*. In some cases—as in "Before I knocked"—religious imagery informs the poetic language and directs the reader to the substantive topic of the poem; in other cases—"The force that through the green fuse drives the flower" is an example—the religious metaphor, secreted in such phrases as "the hanging man" or "time has ticked a heaven round the stars," adds a coordinate dimension to a poem that is not specifically religious in its topic. But no poem in this first volume is free of some element of this imagery.

Selecting various poetic languages for the differing pieces in *Twenty-five Poems*, Thomas seemed concerned with separating religious and nonreligious matters. The unity of language characterizing *18 Poems*—the particular fusion of sexual, religious, cosmic, literary, and genetic metaphor that Thomas fashioned into poetry—begins to resolve into component languages in this second volume. In the religious dimension, three categories are immediately distinguishable. There are those poems, such as "I, in my intricate image" and "Then was my neophyte," written in a style very similar to that of the eighteen earlier poems. There are others, such as "And death shall have no dominion" and "This bread I break," that, taking religious matters as their primary topic, employ relatively unambiguous syntax and clearly religious imagery. A third group, essentially devoid of religious imagery, addresses secular concerns:

examples are "Hold hard, these ancient minutes in the cuckoo's month" and "Ears in the turrets hear." Some of the best poems in this volume belong to this category; for, no longer finding divinity in all things equally, Thomas sharpened his apprehension of both the religious and the secular by keeping them, and their respective languages, separate.

The poems of religious intent that appear in this volume are not among Thomas' best. They are of interest either as developments from an earlier style or as prototypes of a later. For the former reason, "Today, this insect" (pp. 47-48) deserves attention. A well-wrought poem, it distills from his earlier style the quintessence of verbal density and stands as a poetic commentary on that style. Its twenty-six lines are thick with referential and allusive images: Eden, Genesis, Jericho, John, Job, and Adam are named, while "plague of fables" and "cross of tales" suggest, respectively, Old and New Testament narrative. Yet the topic of "Today, this insect" is not particularly religious. Ambiguous in the extreme and referential in excess, this poem addresses itself to the poetic problems of ambiguity and religious metaphor. Molding style to thought, Thomas' purposeful excesses cross the border from subtlety into outright confusion; this exaggerated style, in fact, creates an instructive self-parody. The poem, a "plague of fables," is certainly plagued with Biblical fable. "This story's monster"—its monstrous confusion— "blows Jericho on Eden": it is the very complexity of the poem that destroys the paradise of fine poetry. Like Eden, a poem (Thomas seems to be saying) is a lovely creation tenanted by beauty. Too much complexity collapses such a structure. Chaos results from the fact that, into such dense rhetoric, almost any meaning may be read: "All legends' sweethearts" have their place in this "tree of stories." The "fable" (the Bible) and the "divided sense" (ambiguity) that are the subject here are features of Thomas' earlier poems; taken together, and exaggerated, they create the "fabulous curtain" of this veiled and impenetrable parody.

For all its religious imagery, "Today, this insect" talks not of religion but about poems that seem to talk of religion. It reflects on his earlier style both in its comments—for it is certainly a poem about poetry—and in its language. As such, it is an instructive example in the development of Thomas' imagery. This parody does not mark the end of his verbal opacities; indeed, not until *Deaths and Entrances* does he achieve a command of style firm enough to produce, consistently, the kind of controlled ambiguity that never topples over into mere confusion. But the parody does mark an awareness of and concern with the problem.

While "Today, this insect" deserves study as a development from an earlier style, several pieces in *Twenty-five Poems* deserve study as prototypes of a later style. "Foster the light" (pp. 69-70) moves through four difficult stanzas of hortatory verse to a fifth, and very much less difficult, stanza:

> Who gave these seas their colour in a shape,
> Shaped my clayfellow, and the heaven's ark
> In time at flood filled with his coloured doubles;
> O who is glory in the shapeless maps,
> Now make the world of me as I have made
> A merry manshape of your walking circle.

God, shaping the world, shaped Adam (the poet's playfellow?) from the clay, and filled the arc of heaven with starry images of Himself just as he filled Noah's ark with pairs of animals. So far, the stanza is simple allusive imagery. In the last three lines, however, exhortation becomes something else. More than prayer, these lines exhibit a consciousness of the poem itself as an act of praise. The poet addresses God, who, as "glory," is both the magnificence and the radiance of the "shapeless maps" of primeval chaos. "Now make the world of me," he prays: asking for superlative blessings ("the world" means "everything" or "a great deal," as in the phrase "I think *the world* of him"), he also asks that God universalize him by fashioning the world out of his clay. As poet, he can understand this process: for he himself, imitating his Creator, has created. Having asked that "Man be my metaphor" (p. 15), and having hit upon the happy definition of poetry as "the sound of shape" (p. 58), he blends art and living in "manshape," a word that expresses the notion of life as something created through art. The "walking circle" of God's creation is man; for manshapes and circles are related here very much as, in "Incarnate devil," the shapes and circles were united by the snake that "stung awake" the "circle" of the world "in shaping-time" (p. 46). Man, walking through life, is for Thomas an embodied cycle whose end is like his beginning. By his craft, Thomas has made a "merry manshape of your walking circle," a cheerful work of art, or piece of praise, out of the God-given materials.

"Foster the light," then, adumbrates the number of later poems that evince a consciousness of the poem itself as an act of praise; it also foreshadows the development of Thomas' thematic images. For the word "manshape" has a thematic sense that goes beyond its denotative elements. Using the previous connotations of "man" and "shape" that have appeared in his poetry, Thomas fashions this word to carry a complexity of meanings. Not fundamentally religious, it does not constitute an example of thematic religious imagery; but it does demonstrate the process whereby certain words or phrases can become significant thematic metaphors.

Another example of a prototype of thematic imagery is "This bread I break" (p. 45). This excellent lyric depends for its religious significance more on the Christian tradition than on the Bible. Here, "bread" and "wine," obvious references to the Eucharist, are also the flesh and blood of the poet, as well as the substance and life of poetry. Form gives an appearance of uncomplicated sense: each compact stanza moves from a consideration of bread and wine to a consideration of destructive man, and each seems restatement of the first. Vocabulary helps create this apparent simplicity: of the poem's hundred words, all but five are monosyllables. Simplicity, however, does not extend to meaning. The words "foreign tree" in the first stanza, and the phrase "Man broke the sun" in the second, suggest the tree of the cross and the crucifixion of the Son. In the immediate context, the presence of the Eucharist helps suggest these interpretations; in a wider context, too, "tree" and "sun" have a thematic value firmly established in Thomas' first two volumes. These meanings being established, the lines "This flesh you break, this blood you let / Make desolation in the vein" come in the third stanza as another allusion to the crucifixion; "let," syntactically meaning "allow to," does double duty in its association with bloodletting, specifically the bloodletting on the cross. "Knocked," a familiar word in Thomas' idiom, suggests the natural processes of sex, prenatal growth, and a desire to escape from surrounding confines. But escape—birth—leads to death. So "Once in this wine the summer blood / Knocked in the flesh" connotes not only the healthy pulse of nature's blood but also the impending destruction consequent on birth, an idea expressed in the connotation of "Knocked in" as "broke in" or "crushed." The third stanza, turning impersonal "Man" into specific "you," also turns the body of Jesus into the body of the poet. The poet's "bread" and "wine"—his real flesh—are in his poems: Thomas seems to address the dismembering critics when he says, "My wine you drink, my bread you snap." Talking of many sorts of destruction—the destruction of Jesus' body by crucifixion, of nature by man, of poet's body by life's process, and of a poem by literary dissection—this poem anticipates Thomas' later style in its simplicity of diction and its central religious metaphor.

A reader unconvinced that "This bread I break" should be treated as more than a simple lyric might well ask what warrant can be produced for such a thorough search of an apparently uncomplicated poem. The warrant is the same that justifies the intense analysis of a thematic image: the warrant of context. Like a thematic image, which owes its substance to themes developed throughout the poet's work, "This bread I break" borrows meaning from its predecessors in *18 Poems* and its neighbors in *Twenty-five Poems*. Like a thematic image, it loses luster when lifted out of the context upon which it rests and by which it is informed. Yet its significance becomes apparent when its individual words are understood in their thematic meanings, and when these ideas about poetry, nature, self, and Jesus are recognized as central concerns in the rest of Thomas' work.

As a poem taking a Biblical matter as its patent subject, "And death shall have no dominion" (p. 77) has a place beside such poems as "Incarnate devil," "This bread I break," and "Altarwise by owl-light." According to Korg, it unifies Thomas' mysticism with accepted Christian doctrine; according to Moynihan, it is no more than a statement of the indestructibility of matter. Whatever it is, it is an anomaly among Thomas' poems. Completely serious in tone, it lacks the humor, irony, or self-awareness of his better work; and its bombastic affirmations fall short of the grand manner of such later poems as "A Refusal to Mourn" or "Poem on his birthday." Notable for an absence of ambiguity, this poem, like a sermon making up in *hwyl* what it lacks in wisdom, takes a verse from Romans (6:9) as its text and illustrates it by examples. The problem seems one of overstatement: to express the Christian idea that death has no dominion, Thomas reaches for monumental figures—constellations, martyrs, and unicorns— as confirmation. What he leaves out is precisely what characterizes all his finest religious statements: an element of personal concern. The expressed sentiment here is undoubtedly in accord with the best Christian principles; what limits the poem is the lack of any hint of commitment to, or faith in, these principles. And faith, no simple thing, can often be expressed only in complex and ambiguous terms. Evidence that Thomas was attempting an unambiguous simplification of this difficult matter may be found in an earlier draft of this poem: the notebook version, adding a stanza to the three published in *Twenty-five Poems*, concludes with the lines "He knows his soul. There is no doubt. / And death shall have no dominion."[1] "There is no doubt"

---

[1] *Notebooks*, p. 188.

perfectly expresses the lack of ambiguity that the reader senses in the published version. And "He knows his soul," whether a wishful thought or a grand self-deception, violates in the extreme the honesty of most of the rest of Thomas' poetry. Deleting the stanza, while it leaves the poem less forthright in its fault, does not solve the problem; for the deleted stanza is just a plainer statement of the ideas that inform the remaining stanzas, ideas that do violence to the central complexity of the religious outlook expressed in the rest of Thomas' work.

"Altarwise by owl-light" (pp. 80-85), the ten-sonnet sequence that ends *Twenty-five Poems*, is one of Thomas' most ambitious poems. Resembling his early work in the range of its Biblical references and the ambiguity of its language, and his later work in its length and humor, this poem also has traditional roots. Like the best sonneteers of English literature—Shakespeare, for example, or Sidney—Thomas takes one particular topic and studies its sundry facets, producing in the process a kind of spiritual autobiography. For Shakespeare and Sidney the topic was the relationship between narrator and lover; for Thomas the topic is the relationship between narrator and Christianity. Like his Elizabethan models, Thomas develops a rough chronology as the sequence progresses: the sonnets at the beginning of "Altarwise by owl-light" concern birth, those in the middle concern growth and the coming of sexual awareness, later ones concern death and the possibilities of resurrection. The sources of metaphor know no limits; Thomas, finding analogies in myth, history, meteorology, geography, cinematography, and even poker, resembles Sidney's ideal poet, "freely ranging only within the zodiac of his own wit."[2] Like his models, too, Thomas finds a major metaphor in writing and language: concerned not only with Christianity, these sonnets also discuss the art of poetry.

Style calls attention to this concern with language, as it did in "Today, this insect." Not primarily parody, however, "Altarwise by owl-light" exhibits Thomas' gymnastic ingenuity at its supplest. With an almost incredible concentration of virtuosity, he unpacks and displays the subtle meanings, puns, and allusive contents of his words, twisting them through a tortuous syntax that wrings out each hidden sense. But it is this very intensity of style that finally contributes to the failure of the poem; for every sense of his words often adds up to nonsense. The proliferation of possible meanings that lends magnificence is ultimately responsible for the diffusion of poetic statement into a fog of distractions and confusions. Ambiguity, in these sonnets, never frees itself from obscurity.

The profusion of religious imagery suggests, as Kleinman argues, that "Altarwise by owl-light" is a fundamentally religious work, and that it proposes some kind of statement about religious matters.[3] Referential imagery abounds here. Adam, Abaddon, Christ, Jacob, Eve, Pharoah, Gabriel, Ishmael, Jonah, Mary, and Peter people the poem, and God, "the Lord's Prayer," "Genesis," "crucifixion," "resurrection," and "that Day" (the

[2] Sir Philip Sidney, *A Defence of Poetry*, ed. J. A. Van Dorsten (London, 1966), p. 24.

[3] *The Religious Sonnets of Dylan Thomas*; for significant alternative readings, see Olson, pp. 63-89, and Tindall, pp. 126-143. For a just assessment of the merits of these three explications, see Korg, pp. 130-132.

*133*

Day of Judgment) all have specific mention. In addition, several clear verbal references point the reader to the poem's Biblical foundations: "Hairs of your head" (Sonnet II) quotes Matthew 10:30, and "My camel's eye will needle through the shrowd" (Sonnet IV) reworks the parable of the rich man entering into heaven.

Allusive imagery is also prevalent. Jesus appears to be the subject of such allusions as "that gentleman of wounds" (Sonnet I), "all glory's sawbones" (Sonnet VIII), and "the tall fish swept from the bible east" (Sonnet X). The cross is a ubiquitous feature of the poem, being variously represented as "a long stick" (Sonnet II), "The horizontal cross-bones of Abaddon" (Sonnet II), and "the rude, red tree" (Sonnet X). Some of the allusions to the crucifixion are clear enough to require little elaboration: "pin-legged on pole-hills" (Sonnet V), "the pin-hilled nettle" (Sonnet VI), and "December's thorn screwed in a brow of holly" (Sonnet X) are of this order. Other allusions involve specific aspects of the crucifixion, or blend crucifixion with other Biblical stories. Sonnet VII begins:

> Now stamp the Lord's Prayer on a grain of rice,
> A Bible-leaved of all the written woods
> Strip to this tree: a rocking alphabet,
> Genesis in the root, the scarecrow word,
> And one light's language in the book of trees.
>
> (p. 83)

Paper, a wood product, forms Bible leaves and becomes "written woods"; but the poet, desiring simplicity and afraid of missing the tree for the woods, takes tree as metaphor for cross and counsels a stripping away of words and a direct apprehension of the meaning of the crucifixion. Jesus, crucified, resembled a scarecrow;

and he produced "one light's language"—a comprehensive and orderly interpretation—to unite and explain the various narratives found in the Bible. The Bible, full of arboreal tales that include the two trees of Eden and the tree of the cross, is "the book of trees." Sonnet VIII, which clearly announces its subject as "the crucifixion on the mountain," ends with an extended allusion:

> I by the tree of thieves, all glory's sawbones,
> Unsex the skeleton this mountain minute
> And by this blowclock witness of the sun
> Suffer the heaven's children through my heartbeat.
>
> (p. 84)

The poet, as a type of Christ, experiences the crucifixion between the crosses of the two thieves. As "all glory's sawbones," he is the supreme healer, and he suffers in order that "heaven's children"—all humanity —may live. "Suffer the heaven's children" also makes a straightforward reference to Jesus' language as reported in the gospels: "Suffer little children, and forbid them not, to come unto me: for of such is the kingdom of heaven" (Matthew 19:14). In this context, the "Blowclock witness of the sun" is an allusion to the "darkness over all the land" (Matthew 27:45) at the time of the crucifixion, as well as an allusion, by way of the pun of "Son" on "sun," to the time-surmounting importance of the Son's sacrifice at this "mountain minute."

While allusive imagery centering upon Jesus commands much of the reader's attention, several other allusive images are worth mentioning. The "bread-sided field" (Sonnet IV) is followed by a mention of the "cutting flood." If this flood is the Red Sea, which cut off the flight of the Israelites until it was cut open to allow a passage and to cut down the pursuing Egyptians (Exodus 14), then the "bread-sided field" suggests the manna that sustained the Israelites after their escape (Exodus 16). The flood appears, here, in the line "Arc-lamped thrown back upon the cutting flood"; as the pun of *ark* on "Arc-" implies, this flood is also an allusion to Noah's deluge. Later, in Sonnet VII, Thomas uses the phrase "house of bread." Possibly suggesting manna, the Biblical allusion here is more probably to "Bethlehem," a Hebrew word which may be translated "house of bread."

This catalogue of referential and allusive imagery—which is by no means exhaustive—still leaves one question unanswered: is this poem a deep and meaningful religious statement? Unlike a number of Thomas' major poems, these sonnets are founded upon neither praise nor prayer: their narrative framework, uncertain though it is, gives the impression of an emphasis on Biblical specifics to the exclusion of religious commitment. The identity of the "I" with several Biblical figures is clear; equally clear is the use of Biblical metaphor to pattern the development of this "I" throughout the course of the poem. But this personal involvement seems to take place on a purely narrative level, as though by a massive assembly of Biblical character and event Thomas sought to cover the lack of any clearly organized and meaningful religious statement. What is needed to balance and inform these referential and allusive images is the kind of depth and integration created by thematic imagery; and thematic imagery is just the ingredient that is absent from this poem. This absence accounts for the lack of certainty that characterizes many of the critical approaches to this poem; for, having nothing as inclusive and integrated as thematic imagery to direct

his interpretation, even the most studious reader, facing
the initial obscurity of this poem, has no real way of
knowing which readings are relevant and which are
absurd. A thematic image, deeply rooted in a poem's
language, has a magnetic effect on the meanings of
other images, tending to polarize and direct them
towards itself. In "Altarwise by owl-light" no single
image stands out as a brilliant compression of the re-
ligious themes of Thomas' poetry.

The one image that comes closest to being thematic
is the one that ends the poem:

> Green as beginning, let the garden diving
> Soar, with its two bark towers, to that Day
> When the worm builds with the gold straws of venom
> My nest of mercies in the rude, red tree.
>
> (p. 85)

Trees, as was noted above, are central images in this
poem: and, in a manner resembling the function of a
thematic image, this final quatrain compresses those
earlier statements into a compact sentence. But—except
for one serious ambiguity—this sentence is simple
enough in its allusions. That the imagery is sexual is
suggested by the lines preceding this quatrain, in which
Peter asks Jesus about his birth. The garden, clearly
Eden, is also Jesus; the "garden diving" that must even-
tually "Soar" is both man's fall and redemption through
Christ, and the crucifixion and resurrection of Jesus.
The "two bark towers" are Eden's two trees; the "Day"
is the Day of Judgment; and the "rude, red tree," by a
pun of "rood" on "rude," is the cross. Trees, gardens,
and worms are all sexual images, and the poem, ending
with a prayer for a female "nest of mercies" to accom-
pany the phallic "rude, red tree," is in one dimension

*137*

simply a sexual statement bolstered by religious metaphor.

But in the dimension of religious statement—which the evidence of referential and allusive imagery reveals as the primary dimension—the central ambiguity of these lines leaves the poem, not with the significance of a thematic image, but with the uncertainty of total ambiguity. "Day," "mercies," "builds," and "gold" all suggest that this final request is for some positive redemptive act, some gesture that can confirm the narrator's commitment to religious faith. But what "builds" is a "worm," emblem of death and duplicity; and what he builds with are "straws," gilded perhaps but nevertheless unsuited for sound construction. Even granting that, since a "nest" is being built, "straws" are acceptable, these are "straws of venom"; for the worm, as serpent, is poisonous, and a serpent's nest, merciful or not, is no desirable occupant of any tree, red or otherwise. If this request is to be taken as a final prayer, it is so equivocal that it seriously undercuts whatever religious statement the poem intends.

Studying the imagery of these sonnets in great detail, Kleinman concludes that this poem is "a deeply moving statement of religious perplexity concluding in spiritual certainty."[4] Perplexity can be granted. Whether or not the poem is "deeply moving" is debatable; but in such matters, perhaps, *de gustibus non disputandum*. The notion that the poem concludes in "spiritual certainty," however, suggests that Thomas wrote from the "There is no doubt" attitude of "And death shall have no dominion." Thomas, like his Biblical namesake, was not free from doubt; what makes his religious statements

[4] *The Religious Sonnets of Dylan Thomas*, p. 10.

remarkable is the absolute honesty with which he addressed himself to, and came to terms with, that doubt. But the terms of any poem, if it is to communicate with its readers, must involve a certain clarity. "Altarwise by owl-light" raises a most serious question about Thomas' terms: how clear was he himself about his statements in this poem? For there is a basic difference between doubt and statements *about* doubt. What critics label "the fallacy of imitative form"—the idea that the best possible expression of ideas about doubt would be a form that leaves the reader doubting—suggests the problem here; for it is, indeed, a fallacy to presume that the best poem about an obscure matter will be an obscure poem.

The distinction between poetic ambiguity and poetic obscurity is found in the care with which a poet has ordered his thought and marshalled his language. That Thomas was capable of writing with a perfectly controlled and ordered ambiguity is proved by his later long poems such as "Vision and Prayer" and "Ballad of the Long-legged Bait." But "Altarwise by owl-light," wanting greater order and discipline than its referential and allusive imagery can give it, lacks the corrective for its obscurity and remains as it initially appears: an intriguing and extravagant failure.

"Here dwell," says Sam Rib in Thomas' short story "The Map of Love," "the two-backed beasts. He pointed to his map of Love, a square of seas and islands and strange continents with a forest of darkness at each extremity."[1] Thomas' third volume, titled after this story, is not unlike this map. Composed of sixteen poems and seven prose pieces—all of which had been previously published in periodicals—*The Map of Love* is organized upon the central topic of love, and is dedicated to Thomas' wife Caitlin. Six of the stories, and most of the poems, address some of the different varieties of love: married and unmarried, happy and distressed, orthodox and perverse, sexual and platonic, divine and secular. While there are some "strange continents" among these poems, most of the "seas and islands" of this part of the map are recognizable. The prose pieces, however, constitute "a forest of darkness at each extremity," and deserve a different sort of study from that given to the poems.

Although this volume, unlike Thomas' previous ones, is unified by a central topic and is presented as a whole rather than as a collection of individual items, many of the poems are among the least successful in *Collected Poems*. Thomas could ply the perfectly fused and blended language of *18 Poems* into many different topics; and the separation of various languages in

[1] *Adventures in the Skin Trade and Other Stories* (New York, 1955), p. 216.

*Twenty-five Poems*, while it created problems, at least allowed him to delve profoundly into a few things. A number of poems in *The Map of Love*, however, bear a curious quality of reintegrated disintegration: it is as though the poet, having analyzed his language into its components, were now seeking to force them back together. The result, to borrow a chemical metaphor, is more a suspension than a solution. Like a whipped mixture of oil and water, these apparently homogenized combinations will, if watched carefully enough and for a long enough time, reveal themselves as unstable unions.

The distinction between types of religious imagery provides an excellent method for studying this disparity of language. Referential and allusive imagery, as they were employed in *18 Poems*, helped develop the Biblical dimension that was part of those poems. Where these types of imagery appeared in *Twenty-five Poems* the primary topic of the poem was often religious; and those poems that did not address a religious subject were cast in a language free from religious imagery. In *The Map of Love*, however, there are a number of poems that, having no distinguishable religious dimension, nevertheless have elements of referential and allusive imagery. "I make this in a warring absence" (pp. 87-89), a poem about a lovers' quarrel presumably between the poet and his wife, is an example. The allusion to Samson, examined earlier, is built out of such lines as "I make a weapon of an ass's skeleton" and "Destruction, picked by birds, brays through the jaw-bone." It is an integral and excellent metaphor for the lover's condition. As is common with allusive images, its value is as fable rather than religious authority. But there occur in the poem a number of other images that seem

*141*

to insist on a religious interpretation: the third stanza has overtones of the conception and crucifixion of Jesus in the words "nettle's innocence," "pigeon's guilt," and "virgins"; in the sixth stanza the word "rood" appears. Taken in conjunction with the Samson imagery, these appear to bring this poem into close association with the Bible, and seem to suggest a religious intent; yet the poem as a whole is devoid of any particularly religious dimension. In the context of Thomas' earlier poetry, such imagery might be expected to signal such a dimension. Here it seems less functional than decorative.

Two other poems of this variety were earlier observed to contain referential and allusive imagery: "How shall my animal," containing the Samson allusion of the "sly scissors" that "Clack through the thicket of strength" (p. 101), and " 'If my head hurt a hair's foot,' " containing the reference "Christ's dazzling bed" (p. 108). In each of these poems statements about secular things —poetry in the former and birth in the latter—are supported by religious imagery. "On no work of words" (p. 104), a poem about the difficulty of writing poetry, uses the word "manna" as a metaphor for something freely and abundantly given. In all three of these poems the images cited stand out as the only religious element present in the language. They support no religious dimension, and apparently are not meant to direct the reader to the Bible.

The problem is that such images *do* direct the reader to the Bible, especially since the context of Thomas' earlier poems seems to insist that there is a pervasive religious dimension to his poetry. For this reason it is especially important that the limits of referential and allusive imagery be understood. If the reader were to presume that all religious imagery functioned equally, and that a religious image always signalled a religious statement, the above-named poems, lacking a religious dimension, might appear confused and obscure. Realizing instead that referential and allusive imagery most frequently signals the *narrative* rather than the *religious* aspect of the Bible, the reader can more easily distinguish between varieties of language.[2]

"A saint about to fall" (pp. 105-107) makes a more integral use of religious imagery than do the four poems mentioned above. The "saint" which is "about to fall" is the unborn child awaiting parturition. Referential and allusive imagery describe his birth. "The stained flats of heaven . . . [were] razed / To the kissed kite hems of his shawl": perfectly ambiguous, these lines mean both that the blemished plains of heaven were raised like the hem of Jesus' garment to the lips of a worshipper (Matthew 9:20), and that the "stained

---

[2] I am aware that this argument seems to fuse referential and allusive imagery into one undifferentiated type, and that the carefully defined distinctions between them that were advanced in previous chapters may appear to have been abandoned. This simplification is in appearance only. The present discussion centers upon the religious dimension of Thomas' poetry in general, and is directed at identifying those poems which have an authentic religious concern and at distinguishing them from those that do not. In such a discussion the major demarcation will fall between the thematic images on the one hand—which are capable of profound religious statements—and the less comprehensive referential and allusive images on the other. But in any discussion of the total meaning of an *individual* poem, the relationship between varieties of poetic language will be of primary interest; in that case the essential distinction between allusive imagery, which unites these varieties of poetic language into one image, and referential imagery, which tends to have a Biblical meaning only, will be of paramount importance.

flats" (apartments) inhabited by "heaven"—in other words, churches with their stained-glass windows—were "razed" or destroyed at his birth. His birth also found "the quick / Cut Christbread spitting vinegar." Cut to the quick, the child, like Jesus, is crucified; this perversion of the Eucharist identifies bread with the substance of Christ but turns sacramental wine into the vinegar offered Jesus on the cross. "Heaven fell with his fall," and the fallen saint is "Lapped among herods." These images express a familiar Thomas theme: prenatal innocence is corrupted by birth, which introduces to the body the "process in the weather of the heart" that leads to death.

The function of these images is to establish a distinct polarity: Christianity, a metaphor for prenatal goodness, is opposed to material destruction and violence, metaphors for the world that the child will encounter after birth. The vocabulary of the last half of the poem describes this world: "bed of sores," "a war of burning brains and hair," "the time-bomb town," "dark asylum," "murdered," "agony," and "horrid / Woe" are only some of the words depicting this brutal existence.

Basically polar, this poem, rather than talking about religion, uses Biblical imagery as metaphor for something else. Its title, and the vocabulary that includes such words as "praise," "angelic," "Hymned," and "holy," might suggest that religion becomes the subject here; in fact, however, "A saint about to fall" resembles such earlier pieces as "Where once the waters of your face" and "In the beginning," poems that also use religious imagery as metaphors for birth.

The poems in *The Map of Love* discussed thus far have in common a use of referential and allusive imagery that is not primarily directed toward religious statement. These poems are essentially developments from Thomas' earlier style. Along with these, however, *The Map of Love* introduces several poems whose religious language departs from this style in a signal manner. These poems, in fact, mark the beginning of a language that Thomas develops into one of the strongest elements of his later poetry: the language of ritual and sacrament.

Ritual was earlier distinguished from sacrament on the basis of the consciousness of a "deeper reality" underlying the words. A ritual is a prescribed form, and ritualistic language in poetry will call attention to such form, whether it be a form of worship, of dance, of social decorum, or whatever. Ritual, as used to describe Thomas' poetry, may be taken to mean language that refers to some form and order of worship. Sacrament, involving ritual, goes farther and calls attention to the poem itself—to the process of poetic creation and to the very words on the page—as a symbol of a deeper religious realm. On those occasions when ritualistic poetry approaches gesture and act, and rises from words about things towards things in themselves, "sacramental" will be a useful description of the process.

The poems that illustrate this new departure are three: "It is the sinners' dust-tongued bell," "Because the pleasure-bird whistles," and "After the funeral." The first is an example of ritualistic language. The second ends on an image that hints at the beginnings of sacramental language. And in "After the funeral," a fine religious poem, the sacramental language is developed into a full-fledged poetic style.

"It is the sinners' dust-tongued bell" (pp. 92-93), instructive as an example of ritualistic language, does not become sacramental.

It is the sinners' dust-tongued bell claps me to churches
When, with his torch and hourglass, like a sulphur
    priest,
His beast heel cleft in a sandal,
Time marks a black aisle kindle. . . .

From this beginning the poem continues in the same
vein; as Elder Olson has observed, "The details add
up to a Black Mass being celebrated, with Satan offi-
ciating as priest, and . . . Time is being compared to
Satan executing this office."[3] The basic analogy here is
familiar, for the ritual of this religion, black and inverted
though it is, is a metaphor for sexual ritual:

I mean by time the cast and curfew rascal of our
    marriage,
At nightbreak born in the fat side, from an animal bed
In a holy room. . . .

Evoking ceremony in almost every line, the vocabulary
of this poem includes "Altar," "candle," "choir," "chant,"
"cathedral," "bell," and many other words depicting
ritual. The result, however, is description rather than
participation. Not written in imitation of a canticle to
be used in a black mass, nor as a spell to be cast over
the marriage bed, this poem is really a conceit. The
extended analogy involves ritual; but the function of
the language is not sacramental.

    "Because the pleasure-bird whistles" (p. 86), lacking
the concentration and consistency of fine poetry, has
fine moments. Originally entitled "January 1939," this
poem is the meditation of an "enamoured man" as he
looks back "at an old year." Llewelyn, Dylan and Cait-

---

[3] *The Poetry of Dylan Thomas*, p. 58.

lin's first child, was born at the end of January 1939. Facing the new and uncertain responsibilities of a family, the poet, suddenly become "An upright man in the antipodes," looks back on his "pleasure-bird" days. Metaphors here include drugs, sexual perversions, and London, in which he had spent "three dark days" during December 1938, and which he described to Watkins as "an insane city."[4] An allusive image of "the salt person" (Lot's wife) connects London and the old year with Sodom and Gomorrah.

> Because there stands, one story out of the bum city,
> That frozen wife whose juices drift like a fixed sea
> Secretly in statuary,
> Shall I, struck on the hot and rocking street,
> Not spin to stare at an old year
> Toppling and burning in the muddle of towers and
>     galleries
> Like the mauled pictures of boys?

Looking backward, heedless of Biblical warning, the poet risks divine punishment.

Plagued by some of the same problems that "Altarwise by owl-light" encountered, this poem mixes so many metaphors that meaning is diffused into conjecture. Tindall calls it a sermon; several commentators ignore it altogether. What it is that Thomas chooses to bless—London, past pleasure, sodomy, or irresponsibility—is unclear; but that a blessing is intended is certain from the final line, "Over the past table I repeat this present grace." Aware that poetry can constitute sacrament, the poet repeats "this present grace"—the poem itself—as a blessing over "the past table" of his former

---

[4] *Watkins*, p. 49.

life. Unfortunately, saying that a poem is a "present grace" does not make it so. The last line, quite out of place, reads like an interpolation from some other poem. Although provided with an allusive religious image, this poem, affirming sacrament, lacks the ritual that is the basis of sacramental poetry.

"After the funeral" (pp. 96-97), the finest piece in this volume, is an excellent poem by any standard. Not superficially religious, it contains no referential or allusive images to attract the reader's eye. Rather, its grand religious tone is conveyed by thematic imagery and by a carefully controlled use of ritual and sacrament.

"After the funeral, mule praises, brays," and the other inanities of a conventional service have all been performed, "a desolate boy"—the poet—"slits his throat / In the dark of the coffin and sheds dry leaves." Instead of tears or blood, he sheds the "leaves" of poetry: for this poem, in the elegiac tradition of Milton's "Lycidas," Shelley's "Adonais," and Yeats' "In Memory of Major Robert Gregory," takes as its subject not only the honored dead but the whole problem of finding a fitting language to speak of the dead. From the beginning, Thomas is certain that his subject is both Ann Jones and poetic diction. One of the commonplaces of elegiac language, and one that Thomas uses frequently, is the idea that no words are good enough—or that the words already written into the elegy must be rejected as inadequate—to express the grief of the poet and the merit of the dead. In line with this commonplace, the poet of "Lycidas" complains that it is futile "To tend the homely slighted Shepherds trade, / And strictly meditate the thankles Muse" (ll. 65-66); and Yeats, ending his elegy on Major Robert Gregory with the same idea, protests that the thought of his friend's death "took all my heart for speech."[5] "After the funeral" engages this commonplace in a salient way. As important for what it rejects as for what it says, Thomas' poem tries and discards many ways of speaking before it settles on a final, acceptable language. This final language is Christian. Before it is reached, however, a number of approaches —the purely poetic, the pagan, and the pantheistic— have first to be examined.

After shunning conventional ceremony—"the teeth in black, / The spittled eyes, the salt ponds in the sleeves" —as an insincere way of coming to terms with death, the poet chooses the consciously poetic language of a conceit and attempts to comprehend death through the power of secular metaphor. The metaphor tried is, as Moynihan observes, that of water. The poet describes his aunt, "dead, humped Ann," as one "Whose hooded, fountain heart once fell in puddles / Round the parched worlds of Wales and drowned each sun." As water on the wasteland of Wales, Ann's heart—her love—brought life, drowning the parching "sun" while flooding the *son* (the poet) with affection. Turning on this image immediately, however, the following lines discard it as inadequate: "Though this for her is a monstrous image blindly / Magnified out of praise; her death was a still drop." Having no light in "the dark of the coffin," nor in this world where "each sun" is "drowned," the poet, with his eyes presumably "tear-stuffed," "blindly" magnifies her image out of a desire to praise. But the image is "monstrous," expanded beyond the true proportion of praise. Her death, a quiet collapse, was "a still drop," a raindrop or teardrop that, because of its spherical shape and its transparency, has the optical power to magnify. Ann as water (the poet continues)

[5] *Poems*, p. 133.

is inappropriate because she herself would not have approved of all these tears: "She would not have me sinking in the holy / Flood of her heart's fame." Her "heart's fame"—the reputation of her love—is "holy": with this word, the metaphor begins to turn from the secular to the religious.

The first religious terms that the poet tries are pagan in nature: "she would lie dumb and deep / And need no druid of her broken body."[6] Rather than having the services of a pagan druid (whose religion would, fittingly, concentrate on her "broken body" rather than on her more spiritual qualities), she would prefer to be left in silence. Trying to come to terms with death, the poet tries these images of pagan religion and poetic silence. Yet neither is satisfactory. The monument must be raised, and silence would prohibit the poetic process of construction. So, leaving behind the magic of the druids, the poet becomes "Ann's bard on a raised hearth." A "bard," no priest, is rather a singer and teller of tales; the word, in fact, is from the Welsh *bardd* (poet) which is apparently related to a Sanskrit word meaning "he praises." Not contented with silence, this bard praises loudly and vociferously:

> But I, Ann's bard on a raised hearth, call all
> The seas to service that her wood-tongued virtue
> Babble like a bellbuoy over the hymning heads,
> Bow down the walls of the ferned and foxy woods
> That her love sing and swing through a brown chapel,
> Bless her bent spirit with four, crossing birds.

[6] According to Frazer, Welsh witches "are reported to have assumed the form . . . of foxes . . ." (*The Golden Bough*, p. 657). Perhaps the "stuffed fox" in the room with the poet is another aspect of this pagan universe.

These lines move magnificently. Her "wood-tongued virtue" (as silent and as natural as trees) will be made to "Babble," and "her love," like the choir and bells of the "brown chapel," will "sing and swing." Like the country of "In country sleep," this country is holy: images from the landscape fuse with those from the chapel and create a pantheistic ritual. The "seas" have their own "service"; the "chapel," like the trunks of the trees in this "woods," is "brown"; the "bellbuoy" swings like the chapel bell. Nature, the old "foxy" gods, and the "brown chapel" are all blended into the Welsh countryside. But the poet is not content to accept pantheism as the ultimate elegiac expression. Moving from nature and through natural religion, these lines end on an authentically thematic image: "Bless her bent spirit with four, crossing birds." The druid was concerned only with her "broken body." In direct contrast, the concern of this "bard" is with her "bent spirit." Recalling Hopkins' Holy Ghost that "over the bent / World broods with warm breast and with ah! bright wings," the blessing here also involves wings.[7] The "four, crossing birds," perhaps doves, may be (according to John Ackerman) the four winged beasts of Revelation 4:6-8 that praise the throne of God.[8] Whatever they are, they make the four-pointed sign of the cross by their crisscross movements, and offer a formal benediction over the dead.

Having tried and rejected secular, pagan, and pantheistic languages, the poet turns to Christian terms. The remainder of the poem concentrates on raising the previous ritualistic language to the level of the sacramental. For this poem, more than a mere collection of

[7] "God's Grandeur," *Poems*, p. 27.
[8] *Dylan Thomas: His Life and Work*, p. 80.

*151*

words, is a thing, a "skyward statue" that is "carved from her" by the poet-sculptor. Imagery develops the analogy of poem and marble monument:

> I know her scrubbed and sour humble hands
> Lie with religion in their cramp, her threadbare
> Whisper in a damp word, her wits drilled hollow,
> Her fist of a face died clenched on a round pain;
> And sculptured Ann is seventy years of stone.

Like the hands with "religion in their cramp," her "fist of a face" is "clenched" in stoic endurance. Her death is not unlike her life: as unbending as marble in her faith, "sculptured Ann" spent "seventy years" of her life as "stone." This stone, perhaps, suggests the rock upon which Jesus founded his church (Matthew 16:18). Yet the poet's attitude towards her version of religion—which need not affect his own personal religious position—has something of an ambiguity about it. The phrase "sour humble hands," and the pun in "Lie with religion," are perhaps not absolute in their praise of Ann. And the idea that, even without the poet's monument, Ann's existence is "stone" has about it the same excellent ambivalence as Shakespeare's description of those who ". . . rightly do inherit heaven's graces": such individuals, ". . . moving others, are themselves as stone, / Unmoved, cold, and to temptation slow" (Sonnet 94).

However the poet feels about Ann's religion, he is clear about the value of his own. Whether or not intentionally echoing Shakespeare, he is equally clear in his conviction that "Not marble not the gilded monuments / Of princes shall outlive this pow'rful rhyme" (Sonnet 55).

These cloud-sopped, marble hands, this monumental
Argument of the hewn voice, gesture and psalm,
Storm me forever over her grave. . . .

"These" and "this" refer to the poem itself, a "hewn
voice, gesture and psalm" that, like a monument, stands
"over her grave." Unlike a monument, this "Argument"
is "forever"; and, also unlike marble, words are active
things that, not just *standing* as a remembrance of the
poet's love for Ann, "Storm" him over her memory for-
ever.

Forever, that is, until the last Judgment,

. . . until

The stuffed lung of the fox twitch and cry Love
And the strutting fern lay seeds on the black sill.

In this climactic thematic image of resurrection through
the power of the word, nature and the natural gods are
brought together and subsumed into the power of
Christianity. "Love" is one of the distinguishing quali-
ties of the Christian God: for, as John writes (I John
4:8), "God is love." The importance of this conception,
and the essential distinction that it makes between
Christianity and other religions, is central to this poem;
it is through love, rather than through secular conceit,
paganism, or pantheism, that the poet comes to terms
with his subject.[9] It is this sort of love that Thomas

[9] Commenting on significance of the Christian conception of
love, Paul W. Hoon writes: "The boldness and loftiness of
John's declaration that God is love . . . can be appreciated only
when compared with other answers men have made to the
question 'What is God?' Certain Oriental religions reply that
God is a changeless unmoved Being engaged in self-contempla-
tion without concern for human life. Pagan religions have deified

evokes to end his elegy. No passive monument, love is an active force; like the "monumental / Argument" of his sacramental poem, this love, more than a word of ritual, brings to life a deep religious reality that has a present and moving power. It is this cry that sets in motion the apotheosis of fox and fern that is a metaphor for the apotheosis of Ann; and it is this poem, rising from a ritual to a sacramental language, that embodies this cry. What "And death shall have no dominion" could only try to explain, "After the funeral" can confirm and demonstrate: the power of Christian love as a way of coming to terms with death. For this poem, more than any other, the title of Thomas' third volume is appropriate: "After the funeral" is a map of Love.

---

fecundity or sexual life force as God. Ancient and modern Hellenism have conceived God as pure Mind, Wisdom, or Beauty. Moralistic religion has conceived God as Righteousness. Ancient and modern science has conceived God as Energy. The insight of Johannine thought . . . surpasses these in defining God's essential nature as love and represents the highest conception of the divine nature man can hold" (*The Interpreter's Bible*, XII [1957], 30).

The major topic of *The Map of Love* was suggested
by its title: most of the pieces contributed to a charting
of love's topography. In *Deaths and Entrances*, too,
title divulges subject. For although the poems in this
fourth volume are not unanimous in their adherence
to one subject, they are patterned by a certain consist-
ency. The subject is that of *deaths* and *entrances*: to
this set of opposites most of the poems are addressed.

It is perhaps true that the words of this title come
from Donne's sermon "Death's Duell": "Deliverance
*from* that death, the death of the *wombe* . . . is an
*entrance*, a delivery over to *another death*."[1] As adapted
by Thomas, these words take on broad metaphoric sig-
nificance. *Death* is life's end, but life includes early poet-
ry, euphoric youth, sexual prowess, and a religious in-
terest that was less than a total commitment. *Entrances*,
the results of such death, are the beginnings of a mature
poetic style, a concern for the ordering and understand-
ing of past youthful and sexual experience, and a sub-
mission to a greater religious commitment. But death
is not without fear, and entrances are not without ap-
prehension, even when the reward for such radical
change is a whole new mode of religious awareness.
As its basic overall subject, this body of poems takes
the remaking of character by the deaths of old things
and the entrances into new; individually, these poems

[1] Quoted by Tindall, *Reader's Guide*, p. 206.

try to come to terms with the poet's past, present, and future as these are seen in the light of this new religious awareness.[2]

The poems in *Deaths and Entrances* that directly discuss this new religious awareness are three in number. The first poem in the volume, "The Conversation of Prayer," introduces the reader to this subject; "Vision and Prayer" is devoted to a thorough development of it; and "Holy Spring," one of the last poems, reconfirms the idea in no uncertain terms.

"The conversation of prayers about to be said / By the child going to bed and the man on the stairs" (p. 111) describes the process (either aloud between man and child or silently within their heads) of planning what is to be said in bedtime prayers. The man goes to "his dying love," and prays for her "In the fire of his care." The child, "not caring to whom in his sleep he will move," has no particular responsibilities to intensify his prayer, and simply prays routinely for "sleep in a safe land." The man, "full of tears," prays for the "love who dies." And, says the poet, it is the man's prayer, offered in the ardor of extremity, that will be answered, while the child "Shall drown in a grief as deep as his made grave." The difference between these two prayers is marked by the word "care": the man

[2] Rather than trying to tread neatly between "the poet" and "Dylan Thomas"—between the man who may or may not have experienced a religious upheaval and the poet, or narrative "I" in these poems, who says that he did—I prefer to take these poems as metaphors. As metaphors, they describe events that could happen in the life of a man in terms of events that happen to a fictive poet in a poem. The evidence of this volume confirms Dylan Thomas as a religious poet; whether or not he should be considered a religious man involves a wholly different order of investigation.

who cares shall have his prayers answered, while the uncaring child shall suffer. His suffering, however, will not leave him as he is: drowned in sleep, he will "mark the dark eyed wave . . . / Dragging him up the stairs to one who lies dead." Inexorably, he will be dragged "up the stairs" to a man's knowledge, where he will find, if he is not as careful as the man, "one who lies dead." The moral is clear: the caring find comfort, while the heedless grieve.

T. S. Eliot, in "Ash-Wednesday" (1930) took up a similar theme: "Teach us to care and not to care," he prayed, asking that we might be taught to care about the right things and to be unconcerned with the rest.[3] That poem, a magnificent poetic expression of Eliot's religious conversion, began with the line "Because I do not hope to turn again"; throughout, Eliot played on the word "turn" as a metaphor for conversion.[4] Thomas, in "The Conversation of Prayer," uses a similar device. The "conversation," which in the second stanza "Turns in the dark," is also a "conversion": both "converse" and "convert" derive from the Latin word *convertere*, meaning "to turn around." Although the relevance of this idea of conversion, if taken out of its context, might appear uncertain, this poem does, in fact, signal a significant turn-around. A familiar theme in Thomas' work to this point has been that childhood's innocence is pure and desirable. Maturity, adulterating such pristine virtue, corrupts. This poem, however, presents the child as one whose imperfect understanding and heedless unconcern render him incapable of the more mature prayers of the man. Incapable of such prayer, he is excluded

[3] *The Complete Poems and Plays: 1909-1950* (New York, 1952), p. 61.

[4] *Ibid.*, p. 60.

from the divine beneficence granted to the adult. The recognition of the superiority of the adult's religious attitudes is thoroughly Christian: "When I was a child," wrote the apostle Paul, "I spake as a child . . . but when I became a man, I put away childish things" (I Corinthians 13:11).

"The Conversation of Prayer" might be described by the title of an early notebook piece: "Poem Written on the Death of a Very Dear Illusion."[5] Involving the death of so dear an illusion, this finished poem is also an entrance into a whole new realm, a realm in which religion is not only an engaging adjunct but an unavoidable integrant of life. Entering this realm, "Vision and Prayer" (pp. 154-165) develops the theme. Twelve stanzas, diamond-shaped in the first (or Vision) half and hourglass-shaped in the second (or Prayer) half, present conversion as confrontation. Faced with a vision of a holy birth, the narrator describes his reaction, offers a prayer, and is overwhelmed by an unexpected result. Few referential or allusive images appear; the vocabulary is simple, and syntax (once missing punctuation marks are supplied) causes no problem. Although questions of interpretation arise, ambiguity is not a central element, for this poem depends less on the delights of conundrums than on the emotional and dramatic investment that the poet makes.

"Who / Are you," the poem begins. The narrator hears, through a wall "thin as a wren's bone," a birth in the "next room"; and, while no answer is given to his initial question, the words "thorn," "crown," "kingdom come," "dazzler of heaven," and "mothering

[5] *Notebooks*, p. 53.

maiden" combine, in the following two stanzas, to suggest the birth of Jesus. Birth in darkness brings light, and light, illuminating evil, terrifies. In his terror, the narrator turns to worship:

> For I was lost who have come
> To dumbfounding haven
> And the finding one
> And the high noon
> Of his wound
> Blinds my
> Cry.
>
> (part I, stanza 4)

The poet, "Crouched bare" in the security of his Savior, experiences "the judge blown bedlam / Of the uncaged sea bottom" (I, st. 5), or the Last Judgment. This first part ends with the words "And I / Die": the vision that he has seen has, in its intensity, caused death.

The prayer that follows this vision is the entrance after death. In this second section, the poem climbs to its dramatic and poetic climax. "In the name of the lost," who are more carnally than spiritually minded and who "glory in / The swinish plains of carrion," the poet prays that the Savior might return to the womb that bore him. Like the timorous women in Eliot's *Murder in the Cathedral,* who "do not wish anything to happen," and who pray for the Archbishop to depart and leave them in their "humble and tarnished frame of existence," the narrator of "Vision and Prayer" wants only to be let alone.[6] Having no understanding beyond his limited sphere, he prays to remain in it, for

---

[6] Eliot, *Poems and Plays,* pp. 180, 181.

> . . . we have come
> To know all
> Places
> Ways
> Mazes
> Passages
> Quarters and graves
> Of the endless fall.
>
> (ii, st. 4)

Choosing death's oblivion rather than the uncertainty of another entrance, his ultimate request is for darkness:

> O in the name
> Of no one
> Now or
> No
> One to
> Be I pray
> May the crimson
> Sun spin a grave grey
> And the colour of clay
> Stream upon his martyrdom
> In the interpreted evening
> And the known dark of the earth amen.
>
> (ii, st. 5)

Carefully proportioned, this penultimate stanza uses its hour-glass pattern to focus on the central "No." But this negation, not final, is reversed in the last stanza. Picking up the notion of conversion and prayer from "The Conversation of Prayer," this stanza begins, significantly, "I turn the corner of prayer." Unwilling though it may be, this turning is a conversion.

I turn the corner of prayer and burn
In a blessing of the sudden
Sun. In the name of the damned
I would turn back and run
To the hidden land
But the loud sun
Christens down
The sky.
I
Am found.
O let him
Scald me and drown
Me in his world's wound.
His lightning answers my
Cry. My voice burns in his hand.
Now I am lost in the blinding
One. The sun roars at the prayer's end.

(ii, st. 6)

The oblivion of stanza 5, and the self-effacement of the
first part of this final stanza, have not been granted.
Everything here converges on the central "I." Contrast-
ing with the final sentence of part i ("And I / Die"),
this equally abrupt central sentence affirms the entrance
after death. Whatever arguments or prayers he offered
to fend off this total spiritual possession were in vain;
for, like the "light from heaven" that blinded Saul at
his conversion (Acts 9:3), "His lightning answers my /
Cry," and he is "lost in the blinding / One." This final
thematic image combines Paul's blindness, Jesus, and
the "high noon" of the crucifixion into the word "sun."
It also depends on form to convey substance. To be con-
sistent with the syllabic construction of the poem, the

*161*

line "One. The sun roars at the prayer's end" should have nine syllables, as does the line "I turn the corner of prayer and burn" that begins the stanza. The word "prayer's," then, is to be read as having two syllables. As such, the word emphasizes the meaning "one who prays."[7] For the "prayer's end" is not only the end of the poem "Vision and Prayer"; it is also the end of the poet who, in the first five stanzas of his prayer, selfishly prayed against the divine will. That poet is dead; in his place is the convert, unwilling but ready to enter into the commitment of this new mode of religious existence.

"Holy Spring" (p. 177) confirms the value of this commitment. This poem, with its three paradigmatic religious images and its concentrated religious vocabulary, is a celebration. What it celebrates is not the familiar Thomas topic of birth, sex, and death, although these are metaphors that enhance the language. The subject here is praise of a different sort: a praise of the very commitment the poet vainly resisted in "Vision and Prayer," the very commitment that caused the man to succeed where the boy failed in "The Conversation of Prayer." The first stanza defines the situation: the poet arises from bed after a bombing raid. The second stanza considers that situation in a singular light. "No / Praise," he says, is to be given to the idea that "the spring time is all / Gabriel and radiant shrubbery." He

---

[7] Thomas apparently thought of the word "prayers" as having, normally, one syllable. For example, "The Conversation of Prayer," which employs an intricate pattern of end rhymes rhyming with internal rhymes, uses "prayers" and "stairs" as rhyming monosyllables:

"The conversation of *prayers* about to be *said*
By the child going to *bed* and the man on the *stairs*. . . ."
(p. 111; italics added)

will not praise a world that can be defined by beautiful images of the Annunciation and blooming spring; nor (if the Gabriel reference is to Daniel 9) will he praise a world whose destruction can be defined and foretold. In fact (responding to the referential character of the image), he will not praise a world—like that of some of his earlier poems, perhaps—which can be complacently categorized through simple reference to Biblical narrative. Instead he praises "hail and upheaval," which "is sure alone to stand and sing," although it might be "only for a last time." He praises, in other words, the disorder and destruction that jar him from his surroundings, that force him from "the husk of man's home," and cause him to turn to praise. Since extremity drives him to this religious act (the poem says), praise be to extremity, for the religious act is desirable. Like the extremity of a "dying love" in "The Conversation of Prayer," this "hail and upheaval" compels an entrance into religious commitment.

Eliot, because he did not hope to turn away from his newfound convictions, said: "I rejoice that things are as they are."[8] Less certain, the poet of *Deaths and Entrances* studied aspects of his past and strove to assimilate them into the tenets of his religious principles. The three poems discussed above are the only ones in this volume that take conversion as an explicit topic. But the concept of rededication to religious principles—or what might better be called a greater awareness of his commitment to these principles—motivates a number of other poems. Submitting to the ineluctable force of his commitment, the poet examines things as they were and things as they should be and attempts to reconcile his old feelings about these things with the

[8] "Ash-Wednesday," *Poems and Plays*, p. 60.

new rationale of his religious awareness. Some of the resulting poems are not unlike those of Hopkins, in whose work Robert Bridges noted (with some distaste, to be sure) certain "efforts to force emotion into theological or sectarian channels," and a "naked encounter of sensualism and asceticism."[9] The analogy is inexact: Thomas was no theologian, nor was he the ascetic that Hopkins was. But these terms suggest the similarity. In Thomas' poetry, the narrative "I" expresses some of the same uncertainties, and makes some of the same attempts to place sensualism and emotion within the pale of religious commitment that so characterize Hopkins' work.

Three of the poems in *Deaths and Entrances*, addressing sexual sensualism, resemble former attempts to unite the languages of sex and religion. "Into her Lying Down Head" follows in the footsteps of Thomas' earlier style. Referential images, to Samson and to Noah, give a Biblical cast to the language and provide metaphors for the subject. But "Love in the Asylum" and "Unluckily for a Death" differ from their precursors. Each, blending sexual and religious imagery, seems to emphasize sex as metaphor for religion, rather than religion as metaphor for sex. The poet of "Love in the Asylum" (p. 119), rejoicing in the thought of sexual experience as an entrance into a religious vision, ends on an image suggestive of the Creation:

> And taken by light in her arms at long and dear last
> I may without fail
> Suffer the first vision that set fire to the stars.

[9] *Poems of Gerard Manley Hopkins,* ed. Robert Bridges, 2nd ed. (London, 1933), p. 96.

"Unluckily for a Death" (pp. 120-122), a complex poem dealing with a number of topics, is basically a rejection of onanism in favor of love. Two symbols are central: the phoenix represents phallic death and rebirth, and the nun, the "woman in shades / Saint carved and sensual," represents the dream-lover conjured up to satisfy "the wintry nunnery of the order of lust / Beneath my life." Both phoenix, a mythical creation, and nun, who must reconcile sensuality and asceticism ("great crotch and giant / Continence"), are in Thomas' idiom unnatural and unhealthy. The natural and healthy is represented by "my true love," which—since the poem was originally titled "Poem (to Caitlin)"—may be taken as the poet's wife. Ceremonial symbols (phoenix and nun) are rejected: for love is a personal experience not between man and "monstrous" ideals but between man and woman. Through this experience of married love the poet will rise to something like the "first vision that set fire to the stars" in "Love in the Asylum"; for this poem ends with the affirmation that "In your every inch and glance is the globe of genesis spun / And the living earth your sons."

Two sonnets in this volume are attempts to dramatize—and so make more real and apprehensible—two Biblical stories that have to do with the poet's religious commitment. "On the Marriage of a Virgin" (p. 141) uses two allusive images to clarify its point. The heroine here is "miraculous virginity old as loaves and fishes"; the line alludes to John 6 and the feeding of the five thousand. Directing the reader to a story of Jesus' works, this first image helps confirm Virgin as Mary. It also suggests both multiplication (John relates how five loaves and two small fishes were made to feed a multitude) and miracle. Continuing, the poet notes

that "the moment of a miracle is unending lightning /
And the shipyards of Galilee's footprints hide a navy
of doves." As in the multiplication of a small amount
to feed a multitude, one miracle provides continuing
enlightenment for generations of individuals who, like
the poet, are affected by it. "Galilee's footprints" alludes
to the story (also in John 6) of Jesus walking on the
water; once again, one miracle multiplies itself. Multi-
plication produces a "navy of doves": uniting an image
of war with an emblem of the Holy Ghost, this phrase
suggests the power of the Holy Ghost to conquer the
recalcitrant (such as the poet is) and to reproduce, by
union with the Virgin, quantities of holiness.

That the second sonnet, "Lie Still, Sleep Becalmed"
(p. 153), directly precedes "Vision and Prayer" is no
accident; for it cameos the longer poem. Although no
references confirm the source, the sonnet seems to take
Mark 4:35-41 as its text. Mark relates how, when Jesus
and the disciples were at sea, a storm arose. Terrified,
the disciples awakened their sleeping master, who set-
tled the tempest. Previously terrified of only the storm,
the disciples now experienced a different sort of aston-
ishment: "They feared exceedingly, and said one to an-
other, What manner of man is this, that even the wind
and the sea obey him?"

In this sonnet, "we" tell the "sufferer with the
wound / In the throat"—Jesus, who spoke the divine
Word and suffered accordingly—to "Lie still, sleep be-
calmed"; in other words, "we" respond in a manner con-
trary to that of the disciples who awakened him. The
storm is awesome:

> . . . we trembled listening
> To the sea sound flowing like blood from the loud
> wound

And when the salt sheet broke in a storm of singing
The voices of all the drowned swam on the wind.

But these passengers, like the poet of "Vision and
Prayer," fear the greater plight of being forced from
old habits into a recognition of divine power. Preferring
rather to suffer the storm than to undergo the turmoil
of conversion, they entreat the sufferer to "Lie still,
sleep becalmed . . . / Or we shall obey, and ride with
you through the drowned." Dramatizing one moment
in the "unending lightning" of Christianity, this sonnet
depicts the situation facing the disciples and, applying
the force of that situation to the case of one not yet
committed to Jesus' way, reverses its outcome.

The Savior that accosts the poet in these poems is
not exactly the Savior accepted by Christian churches.
Addressing himself to the differences, Thomas wrote
"There was a Saviour" (pp. 139-140). This poem em-
bodies a concern that must have been uppermost in
Thomas' unwarlike mind when it was published in
1940: the disparity between the evils of war and the
ideals of religion.[10] Like "After the funeral," this poem
rejects the hypocrisy and unconcern of formalized re-
ligion, and favors a direct appeal to the power of love.
In the churches of the poet's past, children who were
"kept from the sun" to attend Sunday School were pre-

[10] Thomas' attitude towards the war was straightforward and
personal. "*Write soon* and tell me all about the war," he wrote
to Bert Trick in September 1939 (*Letters*, p. 241); "I have only
my feelings to guide me; and they are my own, and nothing
will turn them savage against people with whom I have no
quarrel." And to Rayner Heppenstall he protested war in gen-
eral, "the evil of which is the war itself and not the things it is
supposed, wrongly, to be attempting to exterminate . . ." ("No-
vember 2, 1939," *Letters*, p. 243).

sented with a rare, common, and cruel version of the
"Saviour": they "Assembled at his tongue / To hear
the golden note turn in a groove," to hear the stale
words repeated as by an inhuman phonograph. This
kind of religion—"Half convention and half lie," as
Thomas said in an earlier poem (p. 73)—was helpless
in the face of the depredations of war. Children raised
in it could only confess that

> When hindering man hurt
> Man, animal, or bird
> We hid our fears in that murdering breath.

They had only silence to protect them "when the earth
grew loud / In lairs and asylums of the tremendous
shout." Now, says the poet, all that is left is "yourself
and myself," "Two proud, blacked brothers" who must
watch disaster strike. Had they remained within the
fold of conventional Christianity, they would not have
spent "One lean sigh" over the evil of war; accepting
its presence and ignoring its details, they would merely
have "wailed and nested in the sky-blue wall" of their
church's protection. Now, truly grieved, they "break a
giant tear" for the war's horror. And, separated from
the churches, they turn to love:

> Exiled in us we arouse the soft,
> Unclenched, armless, silk and rough love that breaks all
> rocks.

Like the "stone" of "After the funeral," these "rocks"
may be the rock of Saint Peter, on which Jesus founded
his church. Breaking rocks, this love breaks resistance.
Phallic, this love also suggests the sexual-religious
vision promised in "Love in the Asylum." As Christian
love, this divine power provides Thomas with a way

of coming to terms with what he felt to be a most un-
holy war.

William Moynihan notes that this poem, which is
"One of Thomas's strongest attacks on organized reli-
gion," has been "mistakenly understood as a tribute to
Christianity and Christ." He suggests that the ending
embodies "a form of impassioned humanism" that is
"not a faith in, nor even a praise of the faith of, the
savior 'rarer than radium.' "[11] The poem certainly should
not be interpreted as a praise of conventional religion;
but the opposite interpretation of the poem—as a deni-
gration of the things that Christianity stands for—
seems too harsh. The recognition of the final line's
"love" as a thematic image, an image that builds on
Thomas' earlier use of the word in "After the funeral,"
provides us with a more accurate view: for, in the con-
text of Thomas' work, and especially in the context of
the commitment expressed throughout *Deaths and En-
trances*, the word "love" connotes a good deal more
than simply "impassioned humanism." "There was a
Saviour," in fact, restates a point made in "After the
funeral": Christian love is vastly more important than
conventional religious attitudes. Lacking the ritualistic
and sacramental language, and the immediacy, of
"After the funeral," "There was a Saviour" is a less suc-
cessful statement: perhaps the stanzaic form (borrowed
from Milton's "On the Morning of Christ's Nativity")
interposes too much distance; perhaps the differences
between the churches' and Thomas' own interpretation
of Christianity were not adequately defined. In any
case, the poem represents one more aspect of the strug-
gle from the deaths of the poet's past to the entrances
into greater religious awareness.

[11] *The Craft and Art of Dylan Thomas*, pp. 178-179.

Another aspect of this struggle motivates "This Side of the Truth (for Llewelyn)" (pp. 116-117): the aspect that concerns free will. Dedicated to his son, this poem, which Olson considers one of Thomas' best, is a father's advice to his son. The three stanzas describe the kind of world the son will mature into: a world in which all is, according to Tindall, "predestined, meaningless, and doomed."[12] The boy can choose how he will act: "Good and bad, two ways / Of moving about your death" are the possibilities open to him. Yet, no matter the course chosen,

> . . . all your deeds and words
> Each truth, each lie,
> Die in unjudging love.

Apparently arguing for predestination, these final lines of the poem in fact qualify greatly the notions of a "meaningless" or "doomed" world. The last line, Christian to the core, rises to the level of thematic imagery by its uses of "love" and by the word "unjudging." Christianity admonishes its adherents not to judge, or condemn, one another. "Judge not, that ye be not judged," enjoined Jesus (Matthew 7:1); and, rebuking the Pharisees, he noted that "Ye judge after the flesh; I judge no man" (John 8:15). And Paul pleaded "Let us not therefore judge one another any more" (Romans 14:13). This "unjudging love," triumphant even over the Day of Judgment, will accept every action without condemnation: for the predestination posited here insures that all the son's choices, rather than leading him to his doom, will be governed by a love so powerful that it can rise above his merely worldly notions of good and evil.

[12] *Reader's Guide*, p. 188.

*170*

"This Side of the Truth" advises a boy. "The Hunch-back in the Park" (pp. 123-124) recalls the life of the "truant boys from the town" who, perhaps needing advice, find it in allegory rather than exhortation. As in "This bread I break," uncomplicated diction embodies profound meaning. According to Davies, this poem finds in the description of a childhood figure a metaphor for poet; it is "a parable of the poet's vocation."[13] Korg, going farther, sees the hunchback as one of Thomas' madmen who are "counterparts of the visionary"; for Moynihan, he is a seer who "suffers . . . so that he may create."[14] In the clearly defined realm of the park, the simple, purposeful acts of the hunchback take on a rich archetypal significance. Part of this richness, however, derives from a dimension beyond that of the hunchback-as-poet and hunchback-as-seer metaphors: the religious dimension of hunchback-as-Jesus and hunchback-as-Adam.

No absolute parallel between hunchback and Jesus or Adam informs this poem. But what hints there are suggest that Thomas, intent on making this figure into significant metaphor, cast it in the form of the two archetypes he knew best. Like Adam, this figure is in a park. Like Adam, too, he made himself a mate, a "woman figure without fault" that grew, in his imagination, "Straight and tall from his crooked bones." Like Jesus, whose representation on crucifixes resembles the form of a hunchback, this "solitary mister" is "Propped between trees"—the crosses of the thieves— "Until the Sunday sombre bell at dark" removes him. In imitation of the Eucharist, he eats bread and drinks

[13] *Dylan: Druid of the Broken Body*, p. 4.
[14] *Dylan Thomas*, p. 116; *The Craft and Art of Dylan Thomas*, p. 58.

water. But the bread, eaten "from a newspaper," is perhaps wrapped in the news Jesus brings to the world, and the water, drunk "from the chained cup / That the children filled with gravel," seems generally to represent the bitterness and spite of the world not yet made free by his truths; this is perhaps the cup to which Jesus referred in asking "let this cup pass from me" (Matthew 26:39). The hunchback "Slept at night in a dog kennel / But nobody chained him up"; for, like Jesus, he had no particular home and belonged to nobody. To nobody, that is, except God; and if, for Thomas as for Joyce, dog is God in reverse, the "dog kennel" may either be the sepulcher of Joseph of Arimathaea or the place appointed in heaven for the risen Jesus. Like the uncaring boy in "The Conversation of Prayer" these boys, "Laughing when he shook his paper," ignore the word he brings. The "woman figure without fault," perfect and immaculate, stands "All night in the unmade park" after the hunchback himself has gone; perhaps she represents the lasting force of Jesus' words against the destructive and unmaking influences of the world. After the day of Jesus, the long night follows. But this figure stands to eternity, lasting long after the world disappears, and

> After the railings and shrubberies
> The birds the grass the trees the lake
> And the wild boys innocent as strawberries
> Had followed the hunchback
> To his kennel in the dark.

Like the boy of "The Conversation of Prayer," who sees the inexorable future "Dragging him up the stairs" out of his uncaring state, these "wild boys innocent as strawberries" will eventually follow the hunchback "To his kennel in the dark": a darkness that, while it may simply be death, may also be the metaphorical death preceding religious entrance.

That Thomas, by this time, had mastered the art of directly addressing a religious matter—an art he had not yet perfected in writing "And death shall have no dominion"—is obvious from two excellent examples: "A Refusal to Mourn the Death, by Fire, of a Child in London" and "Ceremony After a Fire Raid." Each of these takes as subject the death by fire of a child during the war, each seeks a poetic way of apprehending and coming to terms with the horror of such a death, and each ultimately arrives at religious terms. But these poems, seeking similar ends, take divergent roads.

One of the propositions behind "A Refusal to Mourn" (p. 112) is that language fails to express the extremity of human experience that is met in death.[15] "A Refusal to Mourn" is patently a refusal: in it the poet, realizing the inability of language to express the subject, manages to convey that very inexpressibility. Refusing to mourn, he builds a greater monument than mourning can. Passing the limits of the expressible, Conrad's Kurtz, in "Heart of Darkness," came close to expressing it by simply saying "The horror! The horror!" Less exclamatory, and having less narrative to build on, Thomas modifies a technique he had earlier tried (and rejected) in "After the funeral": the technique of silence. Never until doomsday, the poet says, will he mourn the child's death: for it in itself had a "majesty" he could not capture in words. The interweaving of imagery, however, makes this poem more complex

[15] See above, p. 92.

than it first seems. The description of the child's burial, as she lies "Robed in the long friends" beside the "unmourning water," involves, perhaps, a Biblical allusion: ". . . man goeth to his long home," says the preacher in Ecclesiastes 12:5, "and the mourners go about the streets." Refusing to be one of these mourners, the poet affirms that he will never mourn until

> . . . darkness
> Tells with silence the last light breaking
> And the still hour
> Is come of the sea tumbling in harness;

for until that time, noise and light and the rest of the world will provide the only adequate monument to the child's death, compared to which the "grave truth" of his poetry would be petty. When that time comes, he will "enter again the round / Zion of the water bead" and the "synagogue of the ear of corn": he will become one with nature. This nature is seen in religious terms. "Zion of the water bead," making a mountain out of a small drop of a universal compound, makes a universal religion from the Judaism of reentering Zionists and the Catholicism of the rosary (as in "the rain telling its beads," p. 182), just as the poet is universalized by becoming one of an infinity of water drops. And, in "synagogue of the ear of corn," the word "synagogue" (derived from a Greek word meaning "to bring together") suggests the numerous grains collected in an ear. Through "ear," the image suggests the aural aspect of religious worship, in contrast to the "silence of the last light breaking." Only after the end of the earth can language, even conventional religious language, be a satisfactory approach to death. Until then, says the poet,

174

I shall not murder
The mankind of her going with a grave truth
Nor blaspheme down the stations of the breath
With any further
Elegy of innocence and youth.

Justifying this refusal is the final line of the poem: "After the first death, there is no other." Perhaps alluding to the same source as that of the line "And death shall have no dominion" (Romans 6:9), this line seems more closely related to Revelation 2:11 ("He that overcometh shall not be hurt of the second death"), or to Shakespeare's sonnet (146) on the soul, which ends with the line "And Death once dead, there's no more dying then." Whatever its source, its manifestly Christian content confirms the religious basis of the poem. It also confirms the futility of mourning, which, by recalling death, is itself a kind of further death. The poet refuses to engage in such murder, preferring to let the fact of death stand as its own unparalleled monument.

The contradiction inherent in the poem is obvious: true adherence to the proposition expressed here would produce no poem at all. In fact, Thomas wrote a poem, and, in fact, the poem tries to come to terms with death through language. As in "After the funeral," the language moves from convention through nature to Christianity in search of satisfactory terms. It is the realization that Christianity embodies not a mourning over death but an understanding of a power beyond death that sparks the poet's realization that true mourning is a refusal to mourn.

"A Refusal to Mourn," although apparently written later than "Ceremony After a Fire Raid," precedes it in *Deaths and Entrances*. In the context of this volume, the order seems eminently sensible. For while "A Refusal to Mourn" confirms mourning as a kind of death, "Ceremony After a Fire Raid" enters upon another sort of language: the language of ritual and sacrament. The language of "A Refusal to Mourn" is that of logical exposition. Having a proposition to express, the poet turned to words whose assembled denotative and connotative meanings would produce, semantically, the statement he desired. The sequence of phrases in this poem depends on logic, for that which comes later takes its meaning from that which comes before. "Ceremony After a Fire Raid" (pp. 143-146) puts language to a different use, a use that depends not only on logic but also on what Eliot called "the beauty of incantation."[16] Here, repetition of words and phrases adds gesture to meaning. And it is through gesture and form—which belong to the ritual aspects of Thomas' language—as well as through semantic statement, that this poem communicates.[17]

Because of the significance of this gesture, no definable proposition can adequately summarize "Ceremony

[16] "Choruses from The Rock," IX, *Poems and Plays*, p. 111.

[17] It can truly be argued that poetry in general depends on its verbal rituals as well as on its semantic meaning, just as it can be argued that dance depends not only on gesture but on a logical narrative structure of the sort that is often presented by its title. However, just as we would find it extraordinary for someone to narrate, verbally, the story presented by the dance while it was in progress, so we should notice the extraordinary effect of a poem in which gesture, or ritual and incantatory significance, is meant to communicate as much or more than the denotations and connotations of the words. For words are normally used semantically, even in poetry; and only infrequently is a poem able to say as much through gesture as it does through content.

After a Fire Raid." Propositions incorporate logic; and when a poem departs markedly from strict adherence to logical exposition in favor of ritual language, nothing but the poem itself can say what the poem is about. Explication can trace threads in the referential and allusive texture of the poem. But these, especially in a poem woven out of ritualistic language, are only tributary aspects. To note that the words

> Forgive
> Us forgive
> Us your death . . .

echo "Forgive us our debts" in the Lord's Prayer, or to describe the straightforward references to Adam and Eve that occupy the second section of the poem, or to note that the lines ending this second section ("Bare as the nurseries / Of the garden of wilderness") seem to allude to Isaiah 51:3 ("he will make her wilderness like Eden, and her desert like the garden of the Lord . . .")— to make these observations is not to account for the power of the poetry. For this power inheres in the "Ceremony" of the poem, the religious celebration that uses words and the sounds of words to call attention to the poem itself as a ritual, a thing, rather than as a statement about a thing.

Ritual language reaches its effulgence in the third and final section of the poem. Part I set the narrative scene in order, and spoke in the first person plural voice of "Myselves / The grievers"; Part II, more homiletic, used the singular "I." This third part, grandly impersonal, must be seen in its entirety to be appreciated.

Into the organpipes and steeples
Of the luminous cathedrals,

Into the weathercocks' molten mouths
Rippling in twelve-winded circles,
Into the dead clock burning the hour
Over the urn of sabbaths
Over the whirling ditch of daybreak
Over the sun's hovel and the slum of fire
And the golden pavements laid in requiems,
Into the bread in a wheatfield of flames,
Into the wine burning like brandy,
The masses of the sea
The masses of the sea under
The masses of the infant-bearing sea
Erupt, fountain, and enter to utter for ever
Glory glory glory
The sundering ultimate kingdom of genesis' thunder.

One dimension of this language evokes scene: a service
for the dead child is being held at a cathedral in the
midst of a burning city. Another dimension—with the
vocabulary of "requiems," "bread," "wine," and "masses"
—establishes the formal Christian worship of this serv-
ice, a service celebrated in such immense proportions
that its bread is a whole "wheatfield" and its mass
refers not only to a service but to the massiveness of the
sea that participates in it. Unlike "And death shall have
no dominion," in which impersonality and monumental
figures combine to produce merely a monstrous simpli-
fication, "Ceremony After a Fire Raid" has another
side to its language. Repetition insists on the ritual
dimension. Three lines beginning with "Into . . . ,"
three beginning with "Over . . . ," and two more be-
ginning with "Into . . ." introduce the device of repeti-
tion. Not identical, the lines in each of these repeated
patterns are parallel in structure and distinct in content.

With "The masses of the sea," however, repetition becomes incantation; and with the line "Glory glory glory" —a line whose repetition provides no accretion of meaning whatever—semantics becomes less important that ritual. The logical order of language that characterized "A Refusal to Mourn" has given way to a paratactic mode that ranges the elements of this final section in coordinate relationships which communicate more by parallel and repetition than by the step-by-step presentations of logic.[18]

[18] Thomas' poetics here resembles that of Hebrew poetry as exemplified by The Book of Psalms. Dependent neither on rhyme nor on strict rhythm, this poetry is based on parallelism. Describing this poetic parallelism in "The Language of the Old Testament" (*The Interpreter's Bible*, I [1952], 227), Norman H. Snaith writes:

"There are three types of parallelism in Hebrew poetry. The first is 'synonymous,' where the statement of the first line is repeated in the second, but with other words:

Thou shalt break them with a rod of iron:
Thou shalt dash them in pieces like a potter's vessel
(Ps. 2:9).

The second is 'antithetic,' where two opposite thoughts are expressed in the two lines, often with exact contrariness:

Weeping may tarry for the night
But joy cometh in the morning (Ps. 30:5).

The third is 'climbing,' where part of the first line is repeated in the second, and something further is added:

The floods have lifted up, O Lord!
The floods have lifted up their voice (Ps. 93:3)."

Clearly, such parallelism remains unimpaired by translation. The repetitions in Thomas' language—those of "synonymous" parallelism in the lines beginning with "Into . . . ," and those of "climbing" parallelism in the lines beginning "The masses . . ."— contribute to the religious tone of the poem by providing a stylistic allusion to Psalms.

*179*

Thomas admittedly wrote for sound as well as for sense. As many who have heard him read his own poetry can confirm, the blend of these two achieves a remarkable balance and produces an extraordinary effect.[19] The poem is less story than script: it contains the skeleton of words that must be fleshed out by the proper reading. Such a reading gives "Ceremony After a Fire Raid" a significance which elevates it from poetry *about* something to poetry that is itself sacramental, that becomes a "symbol of a deeper reality." That reality is religious, and the religion is Christianity. The language of this poem refuses to do what logical language should do: it refuses simply to mean. In "A Refusal to Mourn," Thomas turned to a recognizable Christian statement as a way of overcoming the futility, the "murder," of language. Here, language itself rises from that limitation to direct the reader toward Christianity. In so doing, the language moves from logic to ritual, and the entire poem becomes an act of celebration, a "*Ceremony* After a Fire Raid."

Ceremony of this sort, which calls attention to its language in such a persistent way, is not unlike the attempt to create in a poem a tension between what the poet *says* (semantically) and what the structure of the poem—or the very fact that the poet is writing poetry—may affirm. At its simplest, this is the tension that would be inherent in a statement, made by a poet in a poem, to the effect that poetry is a lie. On a more complex scale, this tension has a place in poems in which the poet tries to recapture the essence of his youth: made into poetry, youth becomes something other than life,

[19] Thomas' reading of this poem is recorded on *Dylan Thomas Reading*, vol. I (Caedmon TC 1002).

and the poet who seeks life while he is engaged in making poems confronts this tension.

This tension is at work in two of the finest pieces in *Deaths and Entrances*: "Poem in October" and "Fern Hill." In these poems Thomas develops the somewhat stiff syllabic verse of such earlier pieces as "I dreamed my genesis," "A grief ago," and "A saint about to fall" into a flowing meter that, resembling free verse and stream-of-consciousness narrative, is in fact a meticulously crafted stanzaic form. Covering an underlying discipline with an apparent ease, these poems have about them a certain *sprezzatura*, a certain offhand grace that saves them from sluggish sentimentality. But beneath this graceful exterior a firm structure of poetic purpose stands; for these poems are serious attempts to come to terms with the remembrances of youth. That youth, which seemed in retrospect so delightfully "green and carefree" ("Fern Hill," p. 178), was, as the poet of "The Conversation of Prayer" well knows, the youth of a boy "not caring" about an understanding of his world in religious terms. In both "Fern Hill" and "Poem in October" the delight of the poet's boyhood is recalled; and in each a significant religious note is interjected as the poet tries to reconcile past innocence with present knowledge.

More by the fact of its being than by its verbal content, "Poem in October" (pp. 113-115) communicates its message: for, as a poem about the poetic act, it takes itself as example. Its narrative is uncomplicated. Celebrating his birthday, the poet takes a morning walk, has a vision of the "true /Joy" of his youth, hears that youth being made over into poetry, and prays that he will be capable of such poetry on his next birthday.

*181*

The first four stanzas locate the place: on an October (autumn) day that is "summery" at the same time that it has a "springful of larks," and that is at once rainy and sunny—a universal day, in fact—the poet leaves "the still sleeping town." It is his "thirtieth year to heaven," and the country around him is holy. Off the "heron / Priested shore" the rows of bowed waves appear to be "water praying." What seems simply to be a descriptive image of a church—"the sea wet church the size of a snail / With its horns through the mist"— actually entails a contrast of the poet's own personal religious feelings with his feelings about formal religion. Like the church in "There was a Saviour," this snail-like institution carries a protective shell to hide itself. Like a snail, too, this church is small and, presumably, slow. Its "horns through the mist" describe the appearance of its towers seen from a distance; but, since a snail's eyes are on hornlike protuberances, this image might suggest that the church stands blindly in the surrounding fog.

The fourth stanza ends

> There could I marvel
> My birthday
> Away but the weather turned around.

With "turned," the important word for conversion and conversation, the two stanzas describing his youth are introduced,

> And I saw in the turning so clearly a child's
> Forgotten mornings when he walked with his mother
> Through the parables
> Of sun light
> And the legends of the green chapels.

The "parables / Of sun light," including the omni-present pun on "Son," combine with "green chapels" to suggest the Christianity of his upbringing. Experiencing again the "wonder of summer," the poet hears this past life become poetry:

> And the mystery
> Sang alive
> Still in the water and singingbirds.

The mystery of this vision of youth "sang alive": singing, it becomes poetry, and yet remains a part of life as well.

As abruptly as the vision came, it departs: the last stanza begins by repeating the words "And there could I marvel my birthday / Away but the weather turned around." Having had the delight of this fleeting vision, the poet turns to the prayer that ends the poem:

> O may my heart's truth
> Still be sung
> On this high hill in a year's turning.

With no idea what "a year's turning" will bring—what kinds of conversions of attitudes or artistry—the poet frankly offers a prayer that this sort of praise may continue in the future.

"Poem in October," then, is a poem about the making of poetry out of youth. The poet focuses on his present condition—through the initial metaphors of location—and then moves to a consciousness of the past in terms of this present. Inherent in the contrast between these two periods is an awareness that the art of poetry is the means for apprehending this past and making it meaningful. Youth, by itself, has no poetic existence. The mature poet—who has, paradoxically, lost the very youth he longs to capture—gives it that poetic existence. In this process he comes to understand the mature "caring" that, separating him from the child, makes it possible for the "mystery" to sing and also to be alive. In his youth he heard the "parables" that form the basis of his mature religion; that this upbringing was influential is evidenced by the fact that the poem about it ends with prayer. In his youth, also, he experienced the delights that his mature poetry expresses; and the form of this poem, with its carefully ordered structure supporting its seemingly casual tale, provides an example of the value of mature artistic care that is similar to the parable of "The Conversation of Prayer."

Having no introduction to place the poet in relation to his art, "Fern Hill" (pp. 178-180) speaks less about poetry and more about youth. The narrator, celebrant of a ceremonious boyhood, is "honoured," a "prince," and "lordly"; he decorates the trees, sings, and plays his horn. "Adam," "holy streams," and "fields of praise" set a religious tone; yet "Time," the deity here, controls the boy's life. Mingling a sense of joy and delight with a sense of regret, this poem, less resolved and more poignant than "Poem in October," concentrates on the child's innocence and lack of understanding. Youth was "green and carefree" and "heedless."

And nothing I cared, at my sky blue trades, that time allows
In all his tuneful turning so few and such morning songs
      Before the children green and golden
      Follow him out of grace,

says the poet, using the vocabulary ("turning," "morning," "songs") of "Poem in October." The regret expressed here, that "time would take me / Up to the swallow thronged loft by the shadow of my hand," and that the child must someday "wake to a farm forever fled from the childless land," is genuine: it is not the result of any failure of the poem to rise above sentiment. But "Poem in October" comes to terms with the possibilities of regret through prayer. "Fern Hill," also ending with three lines introduced by an interjectory "Oh," concludes very differently:

> Oh as I was young and easy in the mercy of his means,
>> Time held me green and dying
>> Though I sang in my chains like the sea.

Because this death leaves no possibility of any future entrances, regret dominates.

As the other side of the coin of "Poem in October," this poem is an experiment in coming to terms with youth in a nonreligious language. Whether or not "Poem in October," because of its greater complexity and its firmer resolution, is the more successful poem is not really a relevant question. The important point is that Thomas, at a time when religious matters had such an apparently personal bearing on the rest of his poetry, could write both these poems. The problem of reconciling his desire for a return to youthful ignorance with his awareness of the value of mature understanding had no simple solution; and the authoritative statement on the subject made by the first poem of this volume is seriously qualified by this final one. *Deaths and Entrances* offers no final resolution. Fundamentally devoted to a study of the poet's awareness of an increased religious commitment, these poems range over a number of subjects and try many approaches in their search for an appropriate poetic language. While the poems are excellent, many are tentative explorations. Only with *In Country Sleep* does Thomas build, out of the findings of these explorations, a consistently religious language.

*In Country Sleep*, as originally published, comprised six poems: "Over Sir John's hill," "Poem on his birthday," "Do not go gentle into that good night," "Lament," "In the white giant's thigh," and "In country sleep." Certain similarities mark these poems. Each is about an individual confronting either the fact of or the threat of death, and each is an attempt to say something meaningful about the confrontation. "Death is all metaphors," asserted the poet of "Altarwise by owl-light" (p. 80) in *Twenty-five Poems* (1936); in *Deaths and Entrances* (1946) death was still a metaphor. But with *In Country Sleep* (1952)—published less than two years before Thomas' death—the fact of physical death seems to present itself to the poet as something more than a distant event. No metaphor, the death that informs the language of these poems cannot be conquered by seeing it as a sign for something else. For *In Country Sleep* is not fundamentally concerned with the death of youth, or the death of an early poetic style, or the death of sexual fantasy. It concerns, quite simply, the poet's own death. These poems come to terms with death through a form of worship: not propitiatory worship of Death as deity, but worship of a higher Deity by whose power all things, including death, are controlled.

Of these six poems, two stand out as distinct in form from the rest. "Do not go gentle into that good night" and "Lament," metrical poems carefully patterned to rhyme schemes, contrast with the syllabic verse of the other four poems. Unlike their neighbors, these two have no poet-in-the-poem who is observer and reporter of an objective scene; one is a grand, controlled meditation, the other a humorous dramatic monologue. While each deals directly with death, the death is not the poet's: "Do not go gentle into that good night" is a poem about a father, and "Lament" a poem about an old man.

Although superficially very different, these two poems should be taken together as opposite poles of a single sphere of thought: the poet's thought about his father. Among the most significant manuscripts in the Dylan Thomas collection of the State University of New York at Buffalo are five pieces of notepaper, all of a size, on which these two poems were developed. The set, ending with a fair copy of "Lament," suggests that "Lament" and "Do not go gentle into that good night" were written together. One page, in fact, begins with eight incomplete lines of the fourth and fifth verses of "Lament" and continues, for the remaining two-thirds of the sheet, with lines, phrases and words that would become part of "Do not go gentle into that good night." In publication, as well as composition, the histories of these two poems are linked: they first appeared in print on consecutive pages of the November 1951 issue of Princess Caetani's *Botteghe Oscure*. Writing to Madame Caetani, Thomas enclosed "Do not go gentle into that good night" and told her that "this little one might very well be printed with it ['Lament'] as a contrast." A postscript confirms the subject of the poem: "The only person I can't show the little enclosed poem to is, of course, my father, who doesn't know he's dying."[1]

[1] "28th May 1951," *Letters*, p. 359.

"Do not go gentle into that good night" (p. 128) honors a man who, in the words of one of Thomas' biographers, was "not so much an agnostic or an atheist as a man who had a violent and quite personal dislike for God."[2] The poem, a villanelle, opens by urging the failing Mr. Thomas to "Rage, rage against the dying of the light." Four following stanzas, playing on the metaphor of light as life, offer the actions of four different sorts of men as examples: "wise men," "Good men," "Wild men," and "Grave men." In deference, perhaps, to Mr. Thomas' feelings, none of these is holy; no crosses, churches, or hymns lurk in the imagery or vocabulary of these verses.[3] If anything, these four examples suggest pagan worship: the "Wild men who caught and sang the sun in flight" recall D. H. Lawrence's Indians, while the "Grave men, near death, who see with blinding sight" seem more nearly seers or astrologers. The final verse, however, enthrones the object of these exhortations in a position almost of deity:

> And you, my father, there on the sad height,
> Curse, bless me now with your fierce tears, I pray.
> Do not go gentle into that good night.
> Rage, rage against the dying of the light.

---

[2] Bill Read, *The Days of Dylan Thomas*, p. 22.

[3] A possible exception may be the words "green bay" in the third stanza ("Good men, the last wave by, crying how bright / Their frail deeds might have danced in a green bay"). A fine but somewhat unexpected image—if "bay" suggests "harbor"— these lines also make sense if "green bay" is seen as a reference to Psalms 37:35: "I have seen the wicked in great power, and spreading himself like a green bay tree." If "green bay" suggests the apparent profusion and proliferation of the wicked, these "Good men" may be tantalized by the notion that, had they too been wicked, their "frail deeds" would have prospered.

In contrast to these four examples, the "father" here is apotheosized to a heavenly status from which he, like the heavenly Father, can "Curse, bless me now." The poet, offering this poem, offers what is in effect a prayer to his father. This father is his own human father, at whose deathbed he, a dutiful son, asks a blessing. It is also, however, the supreme Christian Deity: for this poem, similar in pattern to "After the funeral" and "A Refusal to Mourn," turns from pagan to Christian language for the ultimate consolation and comprehension of death, and asks that this Father "Curse" and "bless" the poet with, respectively, the fact of and the comprehension of this death.

Contrasting with the measured dignity of this villanelle is the boisterous ribaldry of "Lament" (pp. 194-196). Five stanzas detail the libidinous history of the narrator of this dramatic monologue, from his youth as "a windy boy and a bit" to his old age and the "black reward" of his impending death. Recording this poem, Thomas emphasized the five ages of man in these five stanzas by progressively altering his voice from a boy's tenor through the "bright, bass prime" of maturity and on to the quavering, broken tones of an old man.[4] "Lament," in fact, belongs with *Under Milk Wood* in being a script that demands reading aloud. One of the characters of that play provides an apt summary of this monologist's attitudes: "Oh," sighs Polly Garter, mother of many and wife of none, "isn't life a terrible thing, thank God?"[5]

No less irreverent than Polly Garter's "thank God" is the tone of "Lament," which levels at Christian wor-

[4] This poem is recorded on *Dylan Thomas Reading*, vol. II (Caedmon TC 1018).

[5] Dylan Thomas, *Under Milk Wood* (New York, 1954), p. 34.

ship the charges of its blasphemous humor. The boy of the first stanza is "the black spit of the chapel fold" who leers at "the big girls" on "seesaw Sunday nights." In the second stanza he is "the black beast of the beetle's pews"; in the third, "the black cross of the holy house." Defiling holiness with his blackness (the word "black" occurs eleven times in these five stanzas), the narrator delights in the same sort of inversions that characterize a Black Mass. Pouring into his voice all the repugnance and loathing he can muster, Thomas, reading the final stanza, emphasized the disgust of the old man surrounded by the emblems of religious worship: "chastity," "piety," "Innocence," "Modesty," and the rest of the "deadly virtues."

A dramatic monologue is not necessarily autobiography; the "I" in this poem is not simply a surrogate for Dylan Thomas. An indiscriminate attempt to examine Thomas' own life through the lenses of "Lament" would lead to wholesale misinterpretation. Certain features may suggest his life, however; and one of these features is a possible similarity between the old man and the poet's father. Composing the poem, Thomas apparently had his father in mind. The old man of the final stanza, preferring sin to the "deadly virtues" of religion, seems, like Thomas' father, to have "a violent and quite personal dislike for God." "Lament," in fact, seems to be an exaggerated and fanciful answer to "Do not go gentle into that good night" by a man who plans to do anything but that. There, poet advised father. Hardly on a "sad height," and in no position to "bless," the old man in "Lament" shares the father's attitudes and retorts in an appropriate manner.

Why write such a poem? Partly, perhaps, in parody of conventional religion and its platitudes about death.

And partly, too, in an effort to find in humor a means of distancing death. Playing on his father's attitudes, this poem purports to be the words of an old man facing death. Facing it humorously, in cheerful recognition of a wealth of sins, the poet comes to terms with it more ably than he might through a serious Christian approach, especially since such an approach, though befitting Christians like Ann Jones, might seem out of place in honoring Thomas' father.

More overtly Christian in language and attitude, the other four poems of this volume—"In country sleep," "Over Sir John's hill," "Poem on his birthday," and "In the white giant's thigh"—share many similarities.[6] Each

---

[6] Thomas accounted for the similarities among three of these poems—"Over Sir John's hill," "In country sleep," and "In the white giant's thigh"—in his introduction to a broadcast reading: these three, he said, were one day to "form separate parts of a long poem" which would be titled "In Country Heaven." In it, earth's final destruction would be witnessed and wept over by "the countrymen of heaven," who would tell one another their memories of the "places, fears, loves, exultation, misery, animal joy, ignorance, and mysteries" of earth. The poem would be "made of these tellings," and would be "an affirmation of the beautiful and terrible worth of the Earth . . . a poem about happiness." (See "Three Poems," *Quite Early One Morning* [London, 1954], pp. 155, 156, 157.) It is tempting to speculate on what the long poem might have said; but all that exists of it are Thomas' prose comments and some eight and a half stanzas that have recently come to light in the form of several work sheets and a fair copy (recorded on *Dylan Thomas: In Country Heaven—The Evolution of a Poem* [Caedmon TC 1281]). In any case, the fact that such a poem was being planned at this period—and that, like his other late poems, it contains undisguised and frequent reference to what he called in his prose description "The godhead . . . the beginning Word"—evidences once again his increasing interest in the straightforward presentation of religious concerns.

presents the poet, either in the first person or as "he," as an observer and recorder. In each case a scene provides the impetus for the poem: a sleeping daughter, a hunting hawk, a day in Laugharne, and a walk on a hillside all are taken as subjects. Style, too, unites these poems: the syntax, very much in the pattern of "Poem in October" and "Fern Hill," is fluid and easy; sentences tend to be long and graceful; and the lines of these syllabic poems, open and interconnected by similarities of sense and syntax, contrast greatly with the end-stopped lines of much of Thomas' earlier poetry.

Similarities extend to vocabulary as well. Since, from the book's title, the country has something to do with these poems, it is not surprising to discover that names of animals abound: numerous varieties of fish and mammals are mentioned, and the list of birds is truly impressive.[7] Metaphors for the world surrounding the poet, these animals are the intimations of mortality that suggest the process of death working in life: they are the "sparrows and such who swansing" (sing their swan song) in "Over Sir John's hill," and the "Curlews aloud in the congered waves" that "Work at their ways to death" in "Poem on his birthday." The country they inhabit is, according to the poet's proclamation in "In country sleep," a holy country. Not holy in and of itself, it is made holy by the animals' ceremonious actions. In these poems the nightbird "lauds" and foxes "kneel" ("In country sleep"), the "holy stalking heron" bows

---

[7] "In country sleep" refers to goose, gander, raven, "nightbird," robin, roc, rook, cock, nightingale, gull; "Over Sir John's hill," to hawk, "small birds," sparrows, heron, jackdaws, chickens, cranes, hoot owl, cocks, hens; "Poem on his birthday," to cormorants, herons, gulls, curlews, finches, hawks, eagles, wild geese, larks; and "In the white giant's thigh," to curlews, goose, duck, drake, owl, gander.

his head and sings hymns ("Over Sir John's hill"), "steeple stemmed" herons "bless" ("Poem on his birthday"), and the "white owl," in the "thistle aisles," "crossed" the breasts of the "scurrying, furred small friars" ("In the white giant's thigh").

Describing animal actions, however, does not require the language of pantheism. These actions, making country holy, do not suggest an immanent deity flowing through and available in every natural object. They suggest instead that the country is holy because it is sanctified by worship, the worship of a Deity that transcends His creation. Naming that Deity, Thomas comes at last to a candid use of the word "God."[8]

The animals praise God, and so does the poet, for animals provide him with metaphors for his own experience. Recalling animal stories, "In country sleep" alludes to the "hearthstone tales" of Little Red Riding Hood; "Over Sir John's hill" describes the poet as "young Aesop fabling." But fairy tales and Aesop's fables, no child's play, allegorize serious human experience and provide dramatic commentary on it. Thomas' poems, too, while full of animal stories, are directed at a serious end: the praise of God and the comprehension of death. Death, to be conceivable, must be appre-

---

[8] The words "god" and "gods" had been a regular part of Thomas' vocabulary since his early poems. The capitalized "God," however, occurs eight times in Thomas' last eight collected poems (including "Elegy" and "Author's Prologue"), and only four times in all of the earlier poems. In the earlier appearances Thomas handled the word less as a description of the ultimate authority recognized by the poet than as a Biblical reference: in "Incarnate devil," for example, God is a character in the story of Adam and Eve, while in "Altarwise by owl-light" He is one of a number of Biblical figureheads that surround the story of the crucifixion.

hended through language. It comes as no surprise to find that this language is specifically and unequivocally religious. Facing the ultimate question of human life, Thomas sought answers in the praise of God. This praise, unlike his earlier religious poetry, is not simply mediated by referential and allusive imagery; it seems that as Thomas became less reticent about the open use of the word "God," he came to depend less on Biblical imagery and more on direct reference to the Deity. Perhaps this is to say that his conception of God gained a greater definition in his later poems. For it is also a noticeable phenomenon that the ambiguity so commonly associated with praise in his earlier work is absent here, replaced by a forthright acknowledgment of a Deity whose power, attributes, and worship all suggest that He is the Christian God.

The earlier examination of "In country sleep" revealed the thoroughly religious language of that poem: the poet, drawing his metaphor of the Thief from the scriptures, appealed to Christian faith for protection. In a very different way the allusive texture of "In the white giant's thigh" gives Biblical significance to this ceremonious meditation on death. These two poems make their religious statements—and they are without doubt significant statements—through their imagery. In the two remaining poems of this volume—"Over Sir John's hill" and "Poem on his birthday"—the pattern of imagery that Thomas has so carefully constructed in his previous poetry is superseded by a more intense and less ambiguous style, a style apparently committed to as direct statements as are possible about the poet's understanding of God.

"Over Sir John's hill" (pp. 187-189) is a beautiful, well-paced parable of death and destruction. The tale is uncomplicated: the poet, seeing a hawk hunting small birds, meditates on the order of the universe that contains killing hawk and innocent victims. As "The flash of the noosed hawk / Crashes," the poet records that "slowly the fishing holy stalking heron / In the river Towy below bows his tilted headstone." He and this "elegiac fisherbird," facing the scene, build around it a ceremony: "I open the leaves of the water at a passage / Of psalms," says the poet, to the accompaniment of "saint heron hymning."

The significance of the scene, however, is too complex for any paraphrase. Not only bird, the "hawk on fire," engaged in these "shrill child's play / Wars" is a metaphor for an enemy airplane of the kind common in Thomas' earlier poetry. Loaded with bombs, this airplane's "viperish fuse hangs looped with flames under the brand / Wing." And the poet, watching, reads "in a shell / Death clear as a buoy's bell"; in a seashell, that is, but also in a cartridge. The hawk, which "hangs still" in the "fiery tyburn over the wrestle of elms," is also hangman; and "Sir John's just hill," with a "black cap of jack- / Daws," is judge. In the impersonal killings of nature, of war, and of justice, the poet finds a parable about life and the death that must end it. Hawk and victims participate in an inexorable pattern: " 'dilly dilly,' calls the loft hawk / 'Come and be killed,' " and the small birds, "blithely" facing death, cheerfully answer " 'dilly dilly, / Come let us die.' " Like Stephen Dedalus, who thinks "Ineluctable modality of the visible: . . . Signatures of all things I am here to read . . . ," the poet here, facing the signatures of his world, ponders the inescapable logic of the scene and tries to make sense of its brutality and innocence.[9] He and the heron

---

[9] James Joyce, *Ulysses* (New York, 1934), p. 37.

join in a ceremony; and that ceremony, acknowledg-
ing a power greater than theirs, prays for

> . . . the led astray birds whom God, for their breast of
>     whistles,
> Have mercy on,
> God in his whirlwind silence save, who marks the
>     sparrows hail,
> For their souls' song.

Through words, a fit offering is composed. Mediating
between the ineluctable fact of death on the one hand
and the ineluctable presence of God on the other, heron
and poet act as priests for the small birds. The poem
ends with the poet engraving, "Before the lunge of
the night, the notes on this time-shaken / Stone for the
sake of the souls of the slain birds sailing." As in "After
the funeral," the poem itself becomes a monument to
death.

If "Over Sir John's hill" seems, as Tindall would have
it, simply an elegy "for the birds," the following piece
points the significance of the tale and the significance
of the volume as a whole.[10] "Poem on his birthday" (pp.
190-193) marks the culmination of Thomas' religious
poetry. Simple, personal, concerned with the ultimates
of death and religion, this magnificent poem is a su-
preme exultation by one who, moving through the am-
biguities and uncertainties of his earlier work, has at
last evolved an honest and forthright language of
praise. Like "After the funeral" and "Do not go gentle
into that good night," this poem seeks to overcome
death with religious understanding; yet the death faced
is his own, and Thomas, always best when talking about
himself, rises to the occasion. Like "Vision and Prayer,"

[10] *Reader's Guide*, p. 281.

this twelve-stanza poem presents a scene followed by a prayer; but the tone, no longer one of terror, is one of joy. As in "Over Sir John's hill," the poet finds in the animal nature around him parallels of his own experience, and entertains thoughts about the imminent "lunge of the night" that will destroy him. But this poem progresses; and in its course the fear of the imminence of death yields to the conviction of the immanence of God and His power over life.

Significantly, this study of faith begins with a thematic image: "In the mustardseed sun," the opening line, suggests Jesus' simile of "faith as a grain of mustard seed" (Matthew 17:20) "which, indeed," as the teacher had explained previously (Matthew 13:32), "is the least of all seeds: but when it is grown, it is the greatest among herbs. . . ." Under such a sun, the poet is under the influence of this Son; and this spiritual autobiography, taking faith as its subject, proliferates out of the tiny beginnings sown in Thomas' earlier poetry. "In his house on stilts high among beaks / And palavers of birds," the poet "celebrates and spurns / His driftwood thirty-fifth wind turned age." The house is part of biographical fact: the Thomases lived on the sea's edge in Laugharne, in a house that was indeed "on stilts." Midway through the "threescore years and ten" (Psalm 90:10) of man's life, the poet both "celebrates" the occasion of his birthday and "spurns" the accrual of days that has led to it. For this poem is a novelty among Thomas' serious religious poems in one signal aspect: it does not focus on the past. Rejecting the familiar appeals to the stability or capriciousness of youth, Thomas concentrates the language of this poem on the future. The entire poem is cast in the present tense, and its movement, never *away from* the beginning, is always *toward* the end. "Flounders, gulls, on their cold, dying trails" are led towards their demise, curlews "Work at their ways to death," and the poet himself "Toils towards the ambush of his wounds." "In the thistledown fall, / He sings towards anguish," begins the third stanza: in this October (the month of Thomas' birthday) he is thinking not of past summer but of impending fall, both as season and (in the phrase "-down fall") collapse. Watching the herons on the beach below, he sees death inherent in their actions: "Herons walk in their shroud." His perception of the animal life surrounding him catalogues no youthfulness, no past happiness, and no present joy in living. All seems bleak, cold, and difficult; or, as the psalmist sang in the first part of his psalm on the length of life, "all our days are passed away in thy wrath: we spend our years as a tale that is told. The days of our years are threescore and ten; and if by reason of strength they be fourscore years, yet is their strength labour and sorrow; for it is soon cut off, and we fly away" (Psalm 90:9-10).

The first four stanzas establish this ambience. The fifth glances back briefly to "where his loves lie wrecked" in the first thirty-five years. Then it quickly moves to a remarkable image of the future:

> And tomorrow weeps in a blind cage
> Terror will rage apart
> Before chains break to a hammer flame
> And love unbolts the dark
>
> And freely he goes lost
> In the unknown, famous light of great
> And fabulous, dear God.

Readers of Eliot's *The Waste Land* have long been familiar with the plight of the sibyl of Cumae; for as epigraph to his poem Eliot chose a passage from the *Satyricon* of Petronius that describes her. The sibyl, asking for eternal life, forgot to ask for eternal youth, and so grew older and older. Hung in a cage, she wished only to die. Like the sibyl, "tomorrow weeps in a blind cage" in Thomas' poem; hung up simply to age, the poet feels his youth past and his future hopeless. But the change in these lines is abrupt. Moving from classical to Christian reference, the image of helpless imprisonment gives way to an Apocalyptic vision of salvation. The savior, significantly, is "love," the Christian love that will one day release him to be "lost" in the light of God. The poet of "Vision and Prayer," wanting to remain lost, was found. Here the poet, "lost" from his familiar home and circumstances, is perhaps willing "to be absent from the body, and to be present with the Lord" (II Corinthians 5:8); for, as Jesus cryptically observed, "whosoever shall lose his life shall preserve it" (Luke 17:33). In any case, the paradoxes of his existence are those that the Christian must encounter. Lost, he is free; the light, "unknown," is nevertheless "famous"; and God, the "fabulous" figurehead of fables, is at the same time the cherished and personal "dear God."

All these realizations, he knows, will be his in the future. For the present, however, "Dark is a way and light is a place": toiling in the darkness because of faith, the poet envisions his present darkness, or lack of understanding, as a temporal journey, and his goal of illumination (or God) as something spatial and beyond time. Denying the evidence of his merely worldly beliefs by means of the positivity of his religious faith, he offers another seeming paradox: "Heaven that never was / Nor will be ever is always true." Looking to that future, he dreams of that heaven where he might "wander bare / With the spirits of the horseshoe bay" in the company of "blessed, unborn God and His Ghost, / And every soul His priest"; but, jolted from his vision, he remembers that "dark is a long way." And, alone on his dark earth, he turns to prayer.

The prayer comprises the last three and a half stanzas.

> Oh, let me midlife mourn by the shrined
> And druid herons' vows
> The voyage to ruin I must run,

the prayer begins. Yet mourning is as unsatisfactory now as it was in "A Refusal to Mourn"; and the poet is quick to turn to praise instead. "Yet, though I cry with tumbledown tongue," he asks that he might also "Count [his] blessings aloud." The course he chooses is, in fact, that marked out by the psalmist. Psalm 90, turning from despair at the thought of man's troubled life to the comfort of prayer, makes a simple request: "So teach us to number our days, that we may apply our hearts unto wisdom" (90:12). Teach us, that is, to use our time well; and teach us also, in numbering our days, to count our blessings. Leaving mourning behind, the poet concentrates on his blessings and on the magnificence of the future. Spurning the "Cold, dying trails" of animal life, he celebrates instead the future that holds not simply death but a greater understanding of life. No longer caged and hopeless, man is "a spirit in love" who, rising above the "spun slime" of his world, reaches for the "nimbus bell cool kingdom come" of heaven. But beyond these, he counts "this last blessing most":

That the closer I move
To death, one man through his sundered hulks,
The louder the sun blooms
And the tusked, ramshackling sea exults;
And every wave of the way
And gale I tackle, the whole world then,
With more triumphant faith
Than ever was since the world was said,
Spins its morning of praise.

Here is the ultimate expression of the message that began in "The Conversation of Prayer," the message that affirms the value of mature religious knowledge. This knowledge lets him comprehend his world more clearly: the "sun" (as always, "Son"), once a diminutive mustardseed, "blooms" because of this understanding, and the sea, on which he envisioned his "voyage to ruin," is full of praise. More than knowledge, however, this faith, truly religious, is an active force in life. On his voyage he can not only talk about but "tackle" the gales and waves of destruction; and this "triumphant faith" extracts from these encounters not disaster but praise.

Such (the parable reads) is the power of faith, which, though it is like a grain of mustardseed, will remove mountains. Even the seasons come under its power: no longer mired in the darkness of autumn, the poet hears

. . . the bouncing hills
Grow larked and greener at berry brown
Fall and the dew larks sing
Taller this thunderclap spring . . . .

And, turning from animal nature to the study of his fellow men, he is amazed into exclamation at

202

> . . . how
> More spanned with angels ride
> The mansouled fiery islands! . . .

Charting his course among his fellows, no one of whom is an island, he perceives, through the eyes of his "triumphant faith," the world's beauty. The prayer, and the poem, ends on an unequivocal affirmation of faith:

> . . . Oh,
> Holier then their eyes,
> And my shining men no more alone
> As I sail out to die.

The voyage to death is no longer a "voyage to ruin"; for faith, enhancing the life of these "shining men," raises the poet above loneliness and despair. It is no accident that the narrator, beginning in the company of animals, ends in the company of men and angels. Appraising himself through metaphors of animals, he could only conceive of life as survival of the fittest and ultimate doom of all. But, like the poet at the end of "Over Sir John's hill" who prayed for the "*souls* of the slain birds sailing," the poet here turns from a view of man as animal to a view of man as "a spirit in love"; and this view brings him to terms with death. Having learned to pray, he has brought his desires into accord with God's gifts; the result, no longer the terror that ends "Vision and Prayer," is the simple grandeur of religious faith.

## Chapter XII

"The Prayer's End":

A Conclusion

The three types of religious imagery established in this study, while they are inherent in the principles of Thomas' art, were never defined by the poet himself. They are defined by the reader, and are useful only insofar as he can arrive, through them, at an ordered approach to Thomas' poetry. To assume that they can adequately define religious poetry is to assume that religious poetry has a scientific exactness, that it conforms to strict and absolute laws, and that these laws, described categorically, determine what is or is not art. But poetry is not completely amenable to such laws, and the question "What is religious poetry?" cannot finally be answered by any categories.

Categories, however, can delineate the scope of the question. The category of referential imagery helps the reader understand that clear Biblical reference does not define religious poetry. Similarly, the category of allusive imagery lets him see that a complex of Biblical and secular allusions within one image also fails to determine whether poetry is or is not religious.

But it must not be assumed that the third category, that of thematic imagery, marks the simple question and defines the simple answer. It does not. Thematic imagery does not create religious poetry; were it otherwise, a poem would be a thing no greater than the sum of its parts, and the reader would need only find thematic imagery in order to identify the poet's religious statements. This third category does, however, bring the reader closer to the heart of the question. More helpful than the categories of referential and allusive imagery, it provides a useful set of terms with which to phrase the question.

The preceding chapters exemplify both the values and the limits of these categories. In Part II ("The Three-Pointed Star"), almost all of the cited examples of referential and allusive images were drawn from Thomas' first three volumes of poetry. The primary example of thematic imagery, however, was taken from his final volume. Similarly, in Part III ("The Parables of Sun Light"), the words "referential" and "allusive" were more prevalent in the discussions of *18 Poems, Twenty-five Poems,* and *The Map of Love.* The word "thematic" was applied most frequently to images found in *Deaths and Entrances* and, to a lesser extent, to those found in *In Country Sleep.* In fact, the discussion of this last volume moved beyond these categories. Religious concerns inform these last poems; for these poems, in outdoing Thomas' earlier work, finally outrun this method. This fact, far from rendering this method useless, proves its essential value. For the real worth of the method is that it enforces distinctions between substantive religious statements and supporting imagery. These distinctions help the reader avoid two serious errors: the error of overlooking the significance of Thomas' religious concerns, and the contrary error of indiscriminately attributing that significance to everything he wrote. The method, then, allows the reader to order material and draw some conclusions. These conclusions read something like this:

A young poet begins with a desire to apprehend his world through poetry. An essential part—but only a part—of that world lends itself to religion and a religious language; to express the existence of that part, he turns to a convention and draws referential images from Biblical religion. It is not that he has a body of well-formed cognitive ideas that he longs to express but cannot. Instead, he develops his ideas as he develops language; for, in Cassirer's words, he "lives with his objects only as language presents them to him."[1]

The search for greater definition through language leads him to more profound objects of thought, and in his intensity he begins to modify Biblical reference by adding further dimensions to his images. These dimensions embody his perception of a greater order in his world, an order that insists not only that religion is a metaphor for life but that life provides allegories for religion. Concentrating on such allusive imagery, he begins to take over Biblical narrative and language and to make them his own: he begins, that is, to see the world in terms of his imagery, and in so doing he expands the significance of what was once only a part of his world.

In an effort at even greater definition, his language begins to take on aspects of religious ideas that have no specific Biblical foundation in *a* narrative or *an* episode, but are instead suffused throughout Christian thought. Particular words in his vocabulary become freighted with meaning: words such as "sun," or "count," or "judge," or "love." Their meanings result from the use of these words to establish the major themes of the Bible. The more the poet uses thematic imagery, the more the major themes of the Bible become his themes.

[1] *Language and Myth*, p. 28.

Eventually, however, there comes a point at which even thematic imagery, because it is limited to suggestions of Biblical words, is insufficient. The language with which he discovers and expresses religious concerns goes beyond the limits of Biblical words. Taking over the language of Christian thought has led him to think as a Christian. The order he creates out of his impressions is in accord with Christianity, but the words are his own. His most mature poetry, rising above the limits of any fixed categories, culminates in ritual and sacramental expression of religious matters.

Is this poet Dylan Thomas? Hopefully the questions posed by this study of religious imagery will help the reader answer that question for himself. This method raises vital, rather than merely numerous, questions; it permits us to put disordered impressions into useful words. And it contributes, finally, to the "personal explanation of appreciation" that Dylan Thomas defined as the function of criticism.[2]

[2] *Letters*, p. 29.

**ᕦᕤ** *Appendix*

The Tendency Toward
Ambiguity in Thomas'
Revisions

Poetic revision, clearly, is a complex process. There can be innumerable reasons for striking out a word or line; and any attempt to learn a poet's motivation by studying his revisions is likely to lead to a futility of unresolved guesses. The case is no different for studies of revision in religious imagery. It would be naive to assume that, wherever Thomas has expunged religious imagery, the motive has been a desire to avoid obvious statement. But—from a consideration of effect, rather than motive—a contrast of his drafts with his revisions often demonstrates that his poems move away from straightforward religious imagery towards denser, more opaque statements. Sometimes the entire tenor of a piece is changed in its revision; often the emphasis is shifted, with the result that the formulating thought behind the piece becomes harder to identify. Very frequently, the statements deleted are found to be those which, clear in their religious intent, had restricted the lines to a single meaning.

Clear, confining affirmations were never, to Thomas, poetry. In one of his earliest surviving letters (early 1933) he wrote to Trevor Hughes that an artist, unlike an ordinary man, has not only a life in the "outer world" but a life of "inner splendor," of "unseen places clouding above the brain."[1] He continues: "You may think

[1] *Letters*, p. 10.

this philosophy—only, in fact, a very slight adaptation of the Roman Catholic religion—strange for me to believe in. I have always believed in it. My poems rarely contain any of it. That is why they are not satisfactory to me. Most of them are the outer poems. Three quarters of the world's literature deals with the outer world. Most modern fiction does. Some of it, of course, is purely reporting of outer incidents. Not that that need condemn it. Perhaps the greatest works of art are those that reconcile, perfectly, inner and outer." Dissatisfied with "outer" poems, Thomas desired poetry that could apprehend and express the "inner" essence. Yet art, for him, was not simply a matter of making clear statements about this essence; it was a reconciliation. Although working towards a style that could express such religious attitudes as these, he was unwilling to sacrifice excellence by limiting his statements to matters of religion alone.

Clear statements on religious matters belong, as T. S. Eliot discerned in his essay "Religion and Literature," to a poet of "special religious awareness." Eliot observes that "for the great majority of people who love poetry, 'religious poetry' is a variety of *minor* poetry: the religious poet is not a poet who is treating the whole subject matter of poetry in a religious spirit, but a poet who is dealing with a confined part of this subject matter." This sort of poetry is "the product of a special religious awareness," and it "may exist without the general awareness which we expect of the major poet."[2] Although Thomas' best poems do have both "special religious awareness" and "general awareness," he may have been apprehensive about this kind of stricture

[2] *Selected Essays* (London, 1932), pp. 390, 391.

against religious poetry; the desire to avoid the *minor poet* pigeonhole may have induced him to delete some of his plainer religious statements.

Religious matters, however, frequently seem to have provided the initial language and thought for Thomas' writing. Often the evidence of this original impulse survives in early drafts in the form of fairly unambiguous statements: and, often, these statements are absent from the revisions. This trend towards greater ambiguity can be seen in an examination of one of Thomas' short stories and several of his poems.

## 1. "The Tree"

Thomas published his short story "The Tree" in *The Map of Love* (1939).[3] Set in the Jarvis hills, an imaginary district of Wales, the story tells of a child who, searching for secrets, finds one. Misinterpreting his friend the gardener, who loves the Bible and tells him its stories, the child thinks that the elder tree in his garden is "the first tree," the tree that was "in the beginning." This tree, to which the child prays, is invested with a certain magic: at night it has its own star above it, and, although the garden is covered with snow, it alone is bare. The gardener tells of the crucifixion: "So they hoisted him up on a tree, and drove nails through his belly and his feet." On Christmas morning an idiot, who has been begging his way "from the east" through the Jarvis hills, appears in the garden. The child finds him sitting beneath the tree; convinced that the gardener has told the truth, and that his tree is really the "first tree of all," he reenacts the crucifixion. "Stand up

[3] This story has been subsequently republished in *A Prospect of the Sea* and in *Adventures in the Skin Trade and Other Stories* (New York, 1955).

against the tree," the child orders the idiot at the end of the story.

"The idiot, still smiling, stood up with his back to the elder.

"Put out your arms like this.

"The idiot put out his arms.

"The child ran as fast as he could to the gardener's shed, and, returning over the sodden lawns, saw that the idiot had not moved but stood, straight and smiling, with his back to the tree and his arms stretched out.

"Let me tie your hands.

"The idiot felt the wire that had not mended the rake close round his wrists. It cut into the flesh, and the blood from the cuts fell shining on to the tree.

"Brother, he said. He saw that the child held silver nails in the palm of his hand."[4]

Imagery reinforces Biblical allegory. The Christ-like idiot, a humble, compassionate figure, wears a suit given him by a parson. Thomas translates Jesus' words in Matthew 7:8,9 ("For every one that asketh receiveth . . . Or what man is there of you, whom if his son ask bread, will he give him a stone?") to apply to the beggar: "And asking for water, he was given milk." The gardener, who has "the beard of an apostle," tells the child about "the first love and the legend of apples and serpents," and about Bethlehem, which is "Far away . . . in the East."

The story begins with a description of the tower that is part of the house. The child, having never been in the tower, believes it to contain many secrets. As a Christmas gift, the gardener unlocks the door. The tower, symbol of many things, connects the child's search for

[4] *Adventures in the Skin Trade*, p. 107.

knowledge with the other upright symbol, the tree: disappointed because he can find no secrets in the dusty, empty room at the top of the tower, the child brushes the cobwebs from the window and, looking out at the hills to the east, discovers that Bethlehem is "nearer than he expected." Emphasis on the tower balances the central symbol of the tree: this garden, with its tree of life, has a tower of knowledge, knowledge that confirms, for the child, the importance of his tree.

A beautiful, simple narrative with a complexity of meaning, this story cannot be replaced by such a paraphrase. Paraphrase, however, permits contrast between "The Tree" in this version and the story as it originally appeared in *The Adelphi*.[5] The revised version is somewhat shorter; throughout the story, occasional sentences have been deleted. Also deleted are two paragraphs at the beginning. These original paragraphs describe the Jarvis hills and the setting of the house; not until the middle of the third paragraph is the tower introduced. De-emphasizing the tower as significant symbol, these paragraphs introduce the story as a parable of creation, for their language abounds with references to Genesis. The first sentence of this early version reads "In the beginning was the valley under the Jarvis hills, a circle of green and fruitful land." The valley is a "holy place," where the trees stand "like the fingers of prophets"; it is here that "in the beginning a mother gave birth to her son." The growth of this son, the child in the story, imitates the Creation. As he grows, "The earth and sky, that had been mixed together in one vast cloudiness, separated, even as the clouds of his brain" (the separation of heaven and earth, Genesis

[5] ix (December 1934), 143-149.

1:1-10); "There was a sun that came up the sky as he woke, and a moon as he was put to sleep" (the creation of the "greater light to rule the day, and the lesser light to rule the night," Genesis 1:16); "And there was time that told the light to be dark and the dark to be light" ("Let there be lights in the firmament of the heaven to divide the day from the night; and let them be for signs, and for seasons, and for days, and years," Genesis 1:14).[6]

This early version presents the reader immediately with a Biblical parallel. Emphasis is placed on the mother, who "in the beginning . . . gave birth to her son" (in the revision her part is reduced to the "mother's name" that the child bears). Birth of such a son suggests Cain, first-born of Eve and tiller of the ground. Pursuing this parallel suggests that the child as Cain kills the idiot who calls him "Brother." The idiot, friend of mouse and weasel in the early version, resembles Abel, a keeper of animals. He is slain by the child, who uses wire that had been intended to mend a rake: appropriately, the rake is a tool of a ground-tiller. Genesis and crucifixion are intimately connected here, for this is an allegory of the world from its creation through its search for knowledge to its martyrdom.[7] The later

[6] Similarly, the poem "From love's first fever to her plague" (p. 24) depicts growth as progress from a sense of unity ("The sun and moon shed one white light") to a sense of differentiation ("The sun was red, the moon was grey"). In the same poem, Thomas labels this process of differentiation: "What had been one was many sounding minded."

[7] Thomas, seeing the Bible as a whole, frequently uses such compendious imagery. The two ends of the Bible meet, for example, in the line "Abbadon in the hangnail cracked from Adam" (p. 80), where the destroying angel of Revelation (9: 11) is seen as a descendent, through crucified Jesus ("the

version of "The Tree," emphasizing secular tower instead of Biblical beginning, tells a similar story in more uncertain terms. Revision, while it tightens the story, disguises the allegorical framework and produces a more ambiguous statement.

2. "Our eunuch dreams" (pp. 16-18)

Not overtly religious, this elaborate metaphor of dreams and movies asks, in its third stanza, "Which is the world?" and answers, in the fourth, "This is the world. Have faith." Faith, apparently, suggested an over-simplified optimism to Thomas; the imperative "Have faith" may have seemed too blunt. For, after Geoffrey Grigson had accepted the poem for publication, Thomas wrote to him: "I have been reading over again my poem starting 'Our eunuch dreams,' and am struck more forcibly than before by what might seem to be the jarring optimism of the first six lines of the fourth part."[8] Suggesting a change from "This is the world. Have faith" to "Suffer this world to spin," he noted that the revision sounded "far less false." The letter apparently arrived too late to effect the change, for the poem appeared in its original form in the April 1934 issue of *New Verse*.

By itself, such a change proves nothing. It is significant, however, that Thomas commented on it, and that his revision, spurred by a desire to avoid "optimism," sought to replace an affirmation of positive faith with a statement of indifferent acceptance. His

hangnail"), of Genesis; and the union of birth and death, of Christmas and Easter, reappear in such lines as "My Jack of Christ born thorny on the tree" (p. 15) and "December's thorn screwed in a brow of holly" (p. 85).

[8] "27th March 1934," *Letters*, p. 98.

comment also implies that "Have faith" was not intended as an ironic gesture; irony, often an ingredient in his public statements about faith (as in the prefatory "Note" to *Collected Poems*), rarely colored those made in his poetry.

3. "Foster the light" (pp. 69-70)

Tindall suggests that "this hortatory poem . . . becomes a prayer," as indeed it does.[9] Perhaps, to a reader familiar with Thomas' poetry, prayer is obvious; for, although the poem contains no other explicit Biblical reference, the Being referred to in the lines

> Who gave these seas their colour in a shape,
> Shaped my clayfellow, and the heaven's ark
> In time at flood filled with his coloured doubles,

is most readily identified with God. Proof is in an earlier version. There, the first line quoted above reads "God gave the clouds their colours and their shapes"; revision clouds this clear statement somewhat.[10]

4. "I fellowed sleep" (pp. 31-32)

This poem, about a dreamer flying upwards and surveying his past as he goes, is ancestored by a notebook poem, "The eye of sleep turned on me like a moon." Upward movement, in this earlier draft, brings the dreamer to God:

> There all the matter of the living air
> Raised its harmonious voice; the pulse of God
> Hammered within the circling roads of fire;
> There was the song of God the singing core.[11]

[9] *Reader's Guide*, p. 111.    [10] *Notebooks*, p. 263.
[11] *Ibid.*, pp. 248-249.

The original version ends on an image of confrontation, with the dreamer standing before his Lord's kingdom:

> And stripped I stood upon a columned cloud,
> Fear at my heart of all the laws of heaven
> And the mysterious order of the Lord.
> And, like a bloodred-ribbon where I stood
> There grew the hours' ladder to the sun.[12]

Revision, altering names, changes meanings. Cousin Gwilym in "The Peaches" changed girls' names to God; Thomas, reversing the process, replaces God with father. The revised poem ends, not with dreamer confronting God, but with dreamer facing father. Theology has given place to anthropology.

> There grows the hours' ladder to the sun,
> Each rung a love or losing to the last,
> The inches monkeyed by the blood of man.
> An old, mad man still climbing in his ghost,
> My father's ghost is climbing in the rain.
>
> (p. 32)

In the revised version, the only explicit suggestion that upward movement equals Godward movement is the "angelic gangs" that the dreamer and his fellow pass on their journey. But even these angels, treading "your father's land," have "fathered faces." Father, here, may be God; but it seems more likely, since the context is not particularly religious, that this father is more human than divine.

5. "Incarnate devil" (p. 46)

A notebook poem titled "Before we Sinned," very similar to the published "Incarnate devil," is less com-

[12] *Ibid.*, p. 249.

plex and less ambiguous. In published form the first stanza ends:

> And God walked there who was a fiddling warden
> And played down pardon from the heavens' hill.

God, a violinist, is also an interloper fiddling around in the garden. His "pardon" is "played down"; it is wafted on music down to mortals, but it is also "played down" in the sense of *de-emphasized*. This complexity of language, leading to an ambiguous representation of God, is absent in the notebook version, which reads, quite simply,

> And god walked cool, the ghostly warden,
> And proffered pardon in the ghostly notes
> His robe plucked from the hills.[13]

6. "Do you not father me" (pp. 54-55)

Imagery in this poem centers on house and tower. The tower, in which birds and shells are "babbling," is the Tower of Babel, as well as Freudian image and poetic construction (as in "tower of words," p. 19). Originally, the tower had a further significance: it was the cross. In an early typescript version of this poem— a poem that, when revised, has only a few religious overtones—images of Jesus are associated with tower. Whoever the speaker is—he could be poet, Jesus, new-born child, or the tower itself—he asks, in the original, whether "The bread and vine" is not given for "my tower's sake." He later asks "Am I not all of you?" and includes in this "all" the "towering fish," an image (since Christ is traditionally symbolized by fish) of Jesus on the cross. And, leaving no doubt, the speaker goes on to affirm:

[13] *Ibid.*, p. 199.

Master, this was my cross, the tower Christ.
Master the tower Christ, I am your man.[14]

The published version, hinting at this identification of tower and cross, has only a few explicit religious terms. The words "saviour" and "Abraham-man" appear (although the latter has the simply secular meaning of one who feigns madness); and the tower, "felled by a timeless stroke"—God's eternal wrath?—is described as a "wooden folly," which could be taken as cross. The presence of Jesus, if justified, helps to account for the "grave sin-eater" at the end of the poem. A sin-eater is one who assumes the sins of a dead man; and, in this connection, Jesus is the supreme sin-eater. But the poem has been so altered in revision that such an interpretation, while not at all improbable, is not justified by the material of the poem itself.

These examples could be elaborated; additional ones could be cited. The point, however, is simply that revision, at least in Thomas' early work, tended away from explicitly religious statement and resulted in increased ambiguity of language.

[14] *Ibid.*, p. 349.

## 🦋 Works Cited

*Primary Sources*

Thomas, Dylan. *A Prospect of the Sea and Other Stories and Prose Writings*. London, 1955.

———. *Adventures in the Skin Trade and Other Stories*. New York, 1955.

———. *Dylan Thomas: Letters to Vernon Watkins*, ed. Vernon Watkins. London, 1957.

———. "Poetic Manifesto," *Texas Quarterly*, iv (Winter 1961), 45-53.

———. *Portrait of the Artist as a Young Dog*. London, 1940.

———. "Questionnaire: The Cost of Letters," *Horizon*, xiv (September 1946), 173-175.

———. *Quite Early One Morning*. London, 1954.

———. [Review of *Dictator in Freedom: Tract Four*, by Alfred Hy. Haffenden], *The Adelphi*, ix (February 1935), 317-318.

———. [Review of *The Poems of John Clare*, ed. J. W. Tibble], *The Adelphi*, x (June 1935), 179-181.

———. [Review of *The Solitary Way*, by William Soutar, *Squared Circle*, by William Montgomerie, and *Thirty Pieces*, by Sydney Salt], *The Adelphi*, viii (September 1934), 418-420.

———. *Selected Letters of Dylan Thomas*, ed. Constantine FitzGibbon. New York, 1967.

———. *The Collected Poems of Dylan Thomas*. New York, 1953.

———. *The Notebooks of Dylan Thomas*, ed. Ralph Maud. New York, 1966.

Thomas, Dylan. "The Tree." *The Adelphi,* ix (December 1934), 143-149.

――――. *Under Milk Wood.* New York, 1954.

*Secondary Sources: Studies of Dylan Thomas*

Ackerman, John. *Dylan Thomas: His Life and Work.* Oxford, 1964.

Arrowsmith, William. "The Wisdom of Poetry," *A Casebook on Dylan Thomas,* ed. John Malcolm Brinnin. New York, 1960.

Brinnin, John Malcolm, ed. *A Casebook on Dylan Thomas.* New York, 1960.

――――. *Dylan Thomas in America: An Intimate Journal.* New York, 1955.

Cox, C. B. *Dylan Thomas: A Collection of Critical Essays.* Englewood Cliffs, N. J., 1966.

Daiches, David. "The Poetry of Dylan Thomas," *Dylan Thomas: A Collection of Critical Essays,* ed. C. B. Cox. Englewood Cliffs, N. J., 1966.

Davies, Aneirin Talfan. *Dylan: Druid of the Broken Body.* London, 1964.

FitzGibbon, Constantine. *The Life of Dylan Thomas.* London, 1965.

Fraser, G. S. "Dylan Thomas," *A Casebook on Dylan Thomas,* ed. John Malcolm Brinnin. New York, 1960.

Holroyd, Stuart. "Dylan Thomas and the Religion of the Instinctive Life," *A Casebook on Dylan Thomas,* ed. John Malcolm Brinnin. New York, 1960.

Jones, T. H. *Dylan Thomas.* New York, 1963.

Kleinman, H. H. *The Religious Sonnets of Dylan Thomas.* Berkeley, 1963.

Korg, Jacob. *Dylan Thomas.* New York, 1965.

Lander, Clara. "With Welsh and Reverent Rook: The Biblical Element in Dylan Thomas," *Queen's Quarterly*, LXV (Autumn 1958), 437-447.

Maud, Ralph N. "Dylan Thomas' *Collected Poems*: Chronology of Composition," *PMLA*, LXXVI (June 1961), 292-297.

————. *Entrances to Dylan Thomas' Poetry*. Pittsburgh, 1963.

Moss, Stanley. "Fallen Angel," *New Republic*, June 10, 1967, pp. 19-20.

Moynihan, William T. *The Craft and Art of Dylan Thomas*. Ithaca, N.Y., 1966.

[Obituary]. *Time*, November 16, 1953, p. 93.

Olson, Elder. *The Poetry of Dylan Thomas*. Chicago, 1954.

Read, Bill. *The Days of Dylan Thomas*. New York, 1964.

Saunders, Thomas. "Religious Elements in the Poetry of Dylan Thomas," *Dalhousie Review*, LXV (Winter 1965-1966), 492-497.

Savage, D. S. "The Poetry of Dylan Thomas," *Dylan Thomas: The Legend and the Poet*, ed. E. W. Tedlock. London, 1960.

Shapiro, Karl. "Dylan Thomas," *Dylan Thomas: The Legend and the Poet*, ed. E. W. Tedlock. London, 1960.

Stanford, Derek. *Dylan Thomas*. New York, 1954.

Tedlock, E. W., ed. *Dylan Thomas: The Legend and the Poet*. London, 1960.

Tindall, William York. *A Reader's Guide to Dylan Thomas*. New York, 1962.

*Secondary Sources: General*

Boman, Thorleif. *Hebrew Thought Compared with Greek*, trans. Jules L. Moreau. Philadelphia, 1960.

Brunner, Emil. *Truth as Encounter*, trans. Amandus W. Loos and David Cairns. Philadelphia, 1964.

223

Buttrick, George Arthur, Walter Russell Bowie, Paul Scherer, John Knox, Samuel Terrien, and Nolan B. Harmon, ed. *The Interpreter's Bible*. 12 vols. New York, 1952-1957.

Cassirer, Ernst. *Language and Myth*, trans. Susanne K. Langer. New York, 1946.

Coleridge, Samuel Taylor. *Biographia Literaria*, ed. J. Shawcross. London, 1907.

Conrad, Joseph. *The Nigger of the Narcissus*. New York, 1914.

Crane, Hart. *The Bridge*. New York, 1930.

Cummings, E. E. *Poems: 1923-1954*. New York, 1954.

Eddy, Mary Baker. *Science and Health with Key to the Scriptures*. Boston, 1906.

Eliot, T. S. *After Strange Gods: A Primer of Modern Heresy*. London, 1934.

———. *Selected Essays*. London, 1932.

———. *The Complete Poems and Plays: 1909-1950*. New York, 1952.

Empson, William. *Seven Types of Ambiguity*. 2nd ed. London, 1947.

Fairchild, Hoxie Neale. *Religious Trends in English Poetry*. New York, 1939.

Frazer, Sir James George. *The Golden Bough: A Study in Magic and Religion*, abridged ed. New York, 1922.

Freud, Sigmund. *The Interpretation of Dreams*, trans. James Strachey. New York, 1965.

Gardner, Helen. *Religion and Literature*. London, 1971.

Harvey, Van A. *A Handbook of Theological Terms*. New York, 1964.

Hopkins, Gerard Manley. *Poems of Gerard Manley Hopkins*, ed. Robert Bridges, 2nd ed. London, 1933.

———. *The Poems of Gerard Manley Hopkins*, ed. W. H. Gardener and N. H. MacKenzie, 4th ed. London, 1967.

*224*

James, David Gwilym. *Scepticism and Poetry*. London, 1937.

Jones, David. "Art and Sacrament: An Enquiry Concerning the Arts of Man and the Christian Commitment to Sacrament in Relation to Contemporary Technocracy," *The New Orpheus*, ed. Nathan A. Scott. New York, 1964.

Joyce, James. *Ulysses*. New York, 1934.

Krumm, John McGill. "Theology and Literature: The Terms of the Dialogue on the Modern Scene," *The Climate of Faith in Modern Literature*, ed. Nathan A. Scott. New York, 1964.

Lawrence, D. H. *Apocalypse*. New York, 1966.

Noon, William T. *Poetry and Prayer*. New Brunswick, N.J., 1967.

Robinson, H. Wheeler. *Inspiration and Revelation in the Old Testament*. Oxford, 1946.

Santayana, George. *Interpretations of Poetry and Religion*. New York, 1900.

Scott, Nathan A. *The Broken Center: Studies in the Theological Horizon of Modern Literature*. New Haven, 1966.

———, ed. *The Climate of Faith in Modern Literature*. New York, 1964.

———, ed. *The New Orpheus*. New York, 1964.

Sidney, Sir Philip. *A Defence of Poetry*, ed. J. A. Van Dorsten. London, 1966.

Snaith, Norman H. "The Language of the Old Testament," Vol. I of *The Interpreter's Bible*, ed. George Arthur Buttrick *et al*. New York, 1952.

Stevens, Wallace. *The Collected Poems of Wallace Stevens*. New York, 1954.

Tillich, Paul. *Biblical Religion and the Search for Ultimate Reality*. Chicago, 1955.

Underhill, Evelyn. *Mysticism: A Study in the Nature and Development of Man's Spiritual Consciousness*. London, 1911.

Unterecker, John E. *A Reader's Guide to William Butler Yeats*. New York, 1959.

Watkins, E. I. *Poets and Mystics*. London, 1953.

White, Helen Constance. *The Metaphysical Poets*. New York, 1936.

Wilder, Amos N. *Modern Poetry and the Christian Tradition*. New York, 1952.

————. *The Spiritual Aspects of the New Poetry*. Freeport, New York, 1968.

Wright, G. Ernest. *God Who Acts: Biblical Theology as Recital*. Chicago, 1952.

————. "The Faith of Israel," Vol. I of *The Interpreter's Bible*, ed. George Arthur Buttrick *et al*. New York, 1952.

Yeats, William Butler. *The Collected Poems of W. B. Yeats*, Definitive Edition. New York, 1956.

## ∫∾ Index

Ackerman, John, 3n, 151
*Adelphi, The*, 7n, 12, 95n, 213
Aesop, 194
allusion, in poetry, definition
  of, 52-53
allusive imagery, 51, Chapter
  III *passim*, 95-96, 97, Chap-
  ter V *passim*, 204-205; in
  *18 Poems*, 115, 116, 118,
  120, 122; in *Twenty-five
  Poems*, 126, 128, 134-136,
  138; in *The Map of Love*,
  141, 142, 144-145, 147, 148;
  in *Deaths and Entrances*,
  158, 174, 175, 177; in
  *In Country Sleep*, 195; vs.
  referential imagery, 61,
  63, 108
ambiguity, 126-127, 131-133,
  137-139, 158, 195; and reli-
  gion, Chapter II *passim*;
  and revision, Appendix *pas-
  sim*; vs. obscurity,
  26-27, 34, 139
Arnold, Matthew, 4
Arrowsmith, William, 19n

Bennett, Arnold, 12, 87
Bible books: Acts, 114, 161;
  Corinthians, 88, 89, 158,
  200; Daniel, 48, 163; Eccle-
  siastes, 42, 174; Exodus, 76,
  100, 136; Genesis, 50, 59,
  62, 63, 72-77, 94, 116, 126,

213-214, 215n; Hebrews,
  7, 100; Isaiah, 177; Job, 42,
  50; I John, 153; John, 66,
  94, 97, 102, 119, 165-166,
  170; Joshua, 66; Judges, 63,
  80-84; Luke, 48, 49, 200;
  Mark, 86, 87, 96, 104, 107,
  118, 166; Matthew, 11n,
  50, 87-88, 134, 135, 143,
  152, 170, 172, 198, 212;
  Proverbs, 7; Psalms, 49,
  100-101, 179n, 189n, 198,
  199, 201; Revelation, 37-38,
  105, 115, 151, 175, 214n;
  Romans, 105n, 131, 170,
  175
Biblical figures: Abaddon, 133;
  Abel, 214; Abraham, 23;
  Abram, 50; Adam, 23, 53,
  76, 80, 81, 89, 101, 114, 115,
  120, 126, 127, 133, 171, 177,
  184, 194n; as allusive image,
  71-76, 118; as referential
  image, 59-63, 68; Cain, 214;
  Christ, 5, 40, 41, 52, 65, 89,
  92, 96, 102, 114, 116, 121,
  122, 123, 133, 135, 144;
  Daniel, 48; David, 42;
  Delilah, 64, 65, 82; Eve,
  60-62, 74, 75, 76, 79, 101,
  133, 177, 194n, 214; Ga-
  briel, 48, 49, 51, 56, 133,
  163; Ishmael, 133; Jacob,
  42, 71, 133; Jesus, 11n, 23,